# Rethinking The Modular

T0328067

Edited by Burkhard Meltzer and Tido von Oppeln

Contributions by:
Dimitri Bähler
Lorenzo Bini
Bless
Thomas Dienes
Go Hasegawa
Rem Koolhaas
Thomas Lommée
Wolf Mangelsdorf
Jürgen Mayer H.
Alva Noë
Hans Ulrich Obrist
Nathalie du Pasquier
Rick Poynor
Catharine Rossi
Antonio Scarponi
Jerszy Seymour
Martino Stierli
John Thackara
Georg Vrachliotis
Allan Wexler

With 275 illustrations

 Thames & Hudson

Adaptable Systems in
Architecture and Design

# RETHINKING THE MODULAR

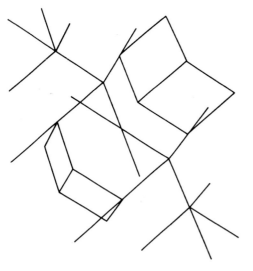

The Systematic                                    17

*Back to the Present*                             24
John Thackara

*An Open Invitation to the Grid*                  32
Thomas Lommée

*There is Always an Alternative:*                 44
*Systems and Production*
Nathalie du Pasquier,
Catharine Rossi,
Antonio Scarponi, Jerszy Seymour

*The Prospects and Limits*                        58
*of Connection*
Rick Poynor

Preface                                            6
*Notes on the 50th Anniversary of*
*USM Modular Furniture Haller*
Alexander Schärer

Introduction                                      10
*Balancing the Modular*
Burkhard Meltzer,
Tido von Oppeln

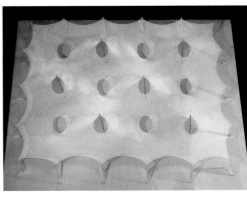

*We Don't Live for a System:*                     70
*New Perspectives for Modular*
*Architecture*
Wolf Mangelsdorf

*How, Then, Does One Organize*                    86
*a City? Fritz Haller's City System*
Georg Vrachliotis

*Working Irrationally*                            104
*with a Rational System*
Allan Wexler

## The Modular 119

*Squaring up to Superstudio:* 126
*Grids, Modularity and Utopianism*
*in Italian Radical Design*
Catharine Rossi

*It's More Like a Service* 154
Bless

*From Functional Object to Icon:* 168
*The Changing Face of the USM*
*Haller System in Advertising*
Martino Stierli

*Dynamic Labyrinth (Seoul)* 188
Rem Koolhaas, Hans Ulrich Obrist

*I Try To Be Architecture* 208
Go Hasegawa

*Wide Minds* 220
Alva Noë

*Calling Someone in China* 236
Dimitri Bähler

*Modularity and Adaptation* 250
Thomas Dienes, Jürgen Mayer H.

*For a Tree, Modularity* 270
*is Not an Issue*
Lorenzo Bini

## Appendix

A Retrospective of USM Haller 284

Contributors' Biographies 291
Photographic Credits 296

# Notes on the 50th Anniversary of USM Modular Furniture Haller

## Alexander Schärer

How do young designers and architects today understand modularity? And how are theorists rethinking the subject of industrialization? The USM Modular Furniture Haller system is now fifty years old. Our company has chosen to mark this jubilee year by founding a cultural initiative with an ambitious goal: 'project50: rethink the modular'.

This book is based on an exchange between more than sixty faculty members, current students and alumni of leading design and architecture schools from around the world: they, along with the participating guest writers and curators, deserve our gratitude for their extraordinary projects and ideas. This temporary academy, known as the USM masterclasses, brought together leading designers and architects who re-examined the concept of modularity through diverse projects. They explored such questions as: What form will the components of modular systems take in the future? To what extent do we view our environment as modular? The work produced through these masterclasses was then exhibited at Milan Design Week, which brought their discoveries to a wider audience. Interviews with these masterclass tutors focus on how their conception of modularity influences their work and how it will shape the design of the future.

Modularity is essentially an idea that came to the fore during the Industrial Revolution. Before that, it was more an intellectual concept than a practical one. Let me give a few examples, only the first of which is pre-industrial:

1.    Religion

Perhaps the ultimate and certainly the oldest modular system, as most of the world religions seem to be modular constructs made up of certain key aspects that combine in sometimes contradictory ways: guilt, redemption, giving life a 'deeper' meaning, providing mechanisms to control adherents and answers to what happens in the afterlife; these are the main building blocks of these systems. All traditional religions use them, and modern cults also try to exploit the same basics, while often pursuing economic aims as well.

2.    'Lego'

Lego, when it was created, was the archetypal modular approach to developing children's skills and imagination. Buildings blocks of different sizes that could be used universally to create almost any toy a child could imagine were produced in enormous quantities and sold all over the world. Unfortunately, in recent years this marvelous idea has been abandoned, as marketing specialists have discovered that they can boost sales tenfold by offering sets that contain much more sophisticated parts, but which allow only one specific toy to be built at a time. Sad for the kids, great for Lego shareholders.

3.    The 'ada' programming language

In the 1980s, some smart researchers tried to create a universal programming language which, for the first time, was not incompatible with its predecessor, but allowed existing algorithms from different sources to be integrated into a form of metacode. The idea was that if various elements had been programmed to deal with certain problems in the past, a modern programmer could integrate these blocks into his program. The idea never took off as expected, apparently because there were never enough of the highly-skilled meta-programmers that were needed to use it. And also, on the bottom line it was cheaper to have entirely new algorithms programmed in emerging countries like India.

4.    And obviously the USM Haller system

While Fritz Haller's modular cities never progressed beyond the conceptual stage and his modular building systems seemed relevant for only a relatively short period, the furniture system is still 'alive and kicking' fifty years after its creation.

Maybe this is sheer luck, or maybe it is due to the numerous enthusiasts, like Paul Schärer, who promoted its worldwide spread. But I think there might be more to it.

First of all, we have to adapt furniture to our needs relatively frequently. When we integrate new technologies or when we move to new premises, let's say. But there is also another aspect: our furniture surrounds us in our everyday lives, so much so that we start to form a certain attachment to it, and this perhaps motivates us, more than financial considerations, to reassemble it in new ways when we move to a new place.

This leads me to a sort of non-conclusive conclusion: even though the Industrial Revolution was the birthplace of the modular concept, over time industrial progress has also become its greatest enemy. Producing with unlimited resources in low wage countries to create ever new products seems to be the smartest and cheapest solution right now. But will that be the case in the long run? I doubt it.

Fritz Haller and Paul Schärer were keen readers of the Club of Rome's *The Limits to Growth* reports. Our generation has lost this almost religious approach to a better life on earth and still exploits our natural resources as if they were unlimited, even though nature seems to be sending us a different message.

The workshop participants who contributed to this project will most likely have to think harder than we have about how to cope with the problems that are arising now and in the future.

And of course I believe, though not in a religious way, that USM Haller still has a great future ahead of it.


Alexander Schärer
President of the Board
USM Holding AG

# Balancing the Modular

**Burkhard Meltzer**
**Tido von Oppeln**

The modular does not have to be invented: it can be found
everywhere. To understand the environment in which we live, we
first divide it into measurable units. In fact, we find it almost
impossible to think of things as a continuum. We divide surfaces
into grids, spaces into pieces, and time into rhythmic units. The
way we perceive and understand the world around us also follows
modular patterns; this is how we make complex structures easier
to grasp. We divide the world into smaller units in order to com-
prehend it and to make future developments more predictable.
Every system begins with measurements and units, and establishing these coordinates gives us a sense of direction and security.
We can rest easy, because systems give us a familiar structure
even in times of change: we continue to recognize repeating
rhythms or patterns.

On the other hand, every day we see evidence that life is not
predictable. Even when we attempt to establish rules, many things
are impossible to foresee. To respond appropriately to changing
situations, we require greater flexibility. Our needs and our living
conditions also change, meaning that parts of our environment—
including even large structures—may be rendered obsolete.

One of the outstanding features of 20th-century architecture
and design up to the 1970s was the application of rational concepts.
Functionalism broke up the objects and spaces we use into

functional units, in order to create more efficient structures in the name of rationalization. In many places this led to industrial standardization, which in the 1960s became known as 'systematic design' or 'systematic architecture'. For better or worse, systematic architecture and Functionalism are still perceived in a particular way, and the minimalist aesthetic of Functionalism still has enthusiastic supporters today—think, for example, of the iPod and iPhone, which deliberately recall designs from the 1960s. By contrast, post-war suburban housing has become a synonym for functional conformity, which tends to imply stagnation and social immobility rather than flexibility and elegance. When we speak of Functionalism and systematic design now, however, we are primarily talking about an aesthetic. Whether or not a device or a building is truly functional is seldom addressed. Nevertheless, the utopia heralded by Functionalism can still be perceived in contemporary items that have their origins in those early designs. The iPhone immediately seems intuitive to use and effortlessly adapted to our needs, and yet everyday experience clearly shows to what extent we have shaped our own behaviour around it.

It was the search for smaller functional units that gave rise to modularity. In essence, modularity means a constant search for, and renegotiation of, the balance between the human need for freedom and flexibility on one hand, and orientation and focus on

Fritz Haller, 'Space Colony', photomontage, 1988

Ettore Sottsass, 'Metafore:
Disegno di un pavimento su cui
i tuoi passi saranno incerti', 1973

the other. Often this cannot be achieved without contradiction or conflict. For example, the units of different systems are rarely interchangeable. Conversely, a module is not only a smaller unit within a system, which can be taken out and put back in the same place: it can also serve as an interface and so communicate with other units and, occasionally, with other systems. A single piece can never be modular, since modularity always implies a connection with other parts. Modular structures are therefore communicative in nature.

Modularity also allows for a connection between the needs for security and growth. The contemporary design and architecture experiments that have emerged from the 'rethink the modular' project are intended to shake up this balance in a productive way. They show what modularity can look like and how it can work. In order to achieve such goals, openness is as vital as a visionary concept: an openness to relationships between different media, materials and locations. In fact, when we speak of the modular, we are already implying a relationship that brings together contrasting or even contradictory elements.

Starting with the communicative potential of the modular, 'rethink the modular' offers two alternative approaches: one involves building new systems, while the other is about changing our perceptions and seeking out modularity within our environment. Sometimes both of these involve making unusual connections; and sometimes they also lead in unexpected directions. 'rethink the modular' attempts to create a dialogue between the postmodern utopia of modular systems and contemporary experiments in design and architecture. The aim of the project is to go beyond the usual topics associated with this kind of modern design, and instead to emphasize its open, communicative and visionary aspects.

This book looks at the work of Fritz Haller (1924–2012), a designer and architect who did not design individual objects so much as networks—pathways and junctions for the interchange of people and information. This visionary quality raises Haller's work to the status of postmodern icons of design and architecture, on a level with Archigram, Superstudio or Memphis. Along with Haller's pragmatic solutions in the field of system architecture, his constructions are also notable for their transcendent beauty. This beauty has the courage to go beyond what is currently possible, daring not only to think the impossible, but to bring it into existence through design.

The utopian vision of a sustainable, flexible living environment was often viewed by postmodernism as a test case for the relationship between territory and real life. According to the architectural theorist Reinhold Martin, 'In postmodernism, Utopia is not only a special kind of territory; it is also another name for the unthinkable.'[1] For him, postmodern utopias primarily mean 'learning to live with Utopia's ghost'. Haller's mega-utopia of the Total City is not meant to be an attainable urban plan for a specific location but an example of modern minds inhabiting a perfectly organized machine. The utopias he drew in such detail are a way of testing the extent to which new methods of communication, faster means of transport and intangible forms of production will radically change both the design profession and the realm of architecture—yet without resurrecting the ghosts of the past or abandoning the utopian potential of architectural design. Haller based the public transport network of his Total City on such models as the architecture of computer chips. In this way, information routes are transformed into transport routes and units of information into a metaphor for the inhabitants of his utopia. The idea of using networks and computer technology to change our world has inspired an entire generation of designers. Just as Haller's Total City suggested a way of living based on the architecture of computer chips, the Memphis series of *Objects for the Electronic Age* sought to find forms that would fit into this unknown future.

In Haller's vision, modular systems are networks that can incorporate a vast range of different dimensions, from USM Modular Furniture Haller to a space station. The latest ideas in contemporary design and architecture are beginning to take up this idea of rethinking the modular. It is now less important that all elements in a system should look the same; the crucial thing is how modules are connected to each other. This book is all about rediscovering the communicative power of the modular.

1   Reinhold Martin, *Utopia's Ghost: Architecture and Postmodernism, Again* (Minneapolis and London: University of Minnesota Press, 2010), p. 151.

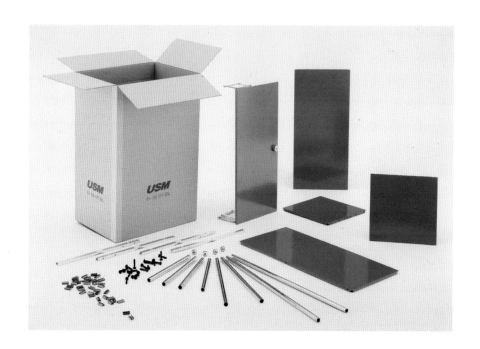

↑ USM Haller modular parts, 1979

← Nathalie du Pasquier, 'Gracieux Accueil', 1983

3

2

4

# THE
# SYSTEMATIC

1

INTERFACE

Allan Wexler

8

STANDARDIZATION

GRID

7                    9

ORGANISMS

1 Ettore Sottsass, 'Systema 45', umbrella stand with ashtray, launched by Olivetti Synthesis, 1973
2 Frei Otto/Larry Medlin, model for a convertible roof, German Pavilion, Montreal, 1964
3 Fritz Haller, 'System with 27 cells', 1968/88
4 Therese Beyeler, aerial photograph of a freeway through a city, 1977
5 Allan Wexler, 'Proposal for Manhattan Skyline, World Trade Center', 1973–76
6 Wolf Mangelsdorf / BuroHappold in collaboration with Zaha Hadid, Riverside Museum, Glasgow, 2011
7 Thomas Lommée's masterclass, 'OpenStructures Relatives', 2014–15
8 Moshe Safdie, Habitat 67, Montreal, view of project from entrance
9 Fritz Haller, public transport system for *Integral Urban: A Global Model*, 1968
10 Jerszy Seymour, 'Coalition of Amateurs', 2009
11 Nathalie du Pasquier, drawing, 2009

11

NGE

FLEXIBILITY

NETWORK

TRANSPORTA

10

EXCHAN

# The Systematic

Back to the Present                 24
John Thackara

An Open Invitation to the Grid      32
Thomas Lommée

There is Always an Alternative:     44
Systems and Production
Nathalie du Pasquier,
Catharine Rossi,
Antonio Scarponi,
Jerszy Seymour

The Prospects and Limits            58
of Connection
Rick Poynor

We Don't Live for a System:         70
New Perspectives for
Modular Architecture
Wolf Mangelsdorf

How, Then, Does One                 86
Organize a City?
Fritz Haller's City System
Georg Vrachliotis

Working Irrationally with          104
a Rational System
Allan Wexler

When we talk about systems in design and architecture, we think of constructing patterns and grids. We instinctively presume that there are clear rules underlying these repeating patterns. In architecture, complex design rules can also embody new social models that aim to create new ways of living and working. Fritz Haller and Paul Schärer had visionary goals of this kind when they developed USM Modular Furniture Haller in the 1960s. Since then, however, the world of work has changed radically. In his essay, John Thackara asks whether future generations could use new modular systems as a sustainable alternative to the machine-age model of growth. Does thinking about systems always involve a search for alternatives, with new social, economical or design implications? A discussion between Nathalie du Pasquier, Catharine Rossi, Antonio Scarponi and Jerszy Seymour explores this question. Rick Poynor looks at the prospects and limits of connection, as well as the interfaces between individual modules and systems. Georg Vrachliotis, meanwhile, discusses utopian urban planning as an example of visionary system architecture for the information society—a background from which the USM Haller system emerged.

Interviews with Wolf Mangelsdorf, Thomas Lommée and Allan Wexler, tutors of the USM masterclasses, discuss new design models and forms of production for sustainable modular structures. As part of the 'rethink the modular' initiative, designers and architects from around the world were invited to think about these topics in a masterclass at the Domaine de Boisbuchet, France, and to develop new projects for an exhibition in Milan.

JOHN
THACKAR

BACK TO THE
PRESENT

# Back to the Present

## John Thackara

Trumpeted as 'the most significant innovation in beekeeping since 1852', the Flow Hive was pitched to a crowdfunding site in 2015 as the beekeeper's dream product. 'Turn the tap and watch as pure, fresh, clean honey flows right out of the hive and into your jar,' gushed the Indiegogo website: 'No mess, no fuss, no expensive equipment—and all without disturbing the bees.' Helped by glowing reviews in *Forbes*, *Wired* and *Fast Company*, Flow Hive's pitch worked like a dream: whereas 70,000 US dollars were needed to launch the product, more than 6 million US dollars had been committed at the time of writing.[1]

Too good to be true? Sadly, yes. As news of Flow Hive spread, natural beekeepers described its approach as 'battery farming for bees'. The modular plastic comb at the heart of Flow Hive's design might well be convenient for honey-loving humans, they charged— but what about the welfare of bees? As Kirsten Bradley explained, the combs in Flow Hive are far more neat and orderly than the ones bees make on their own. Left to themselves, bees set their own cell size according to the season and the colony's particular needs at that moment.[2] A beehive, in other words, is not just a factory:

1   https://www.indiegogo.com/projects/flow-hive-honey-on-tap-directly-from-your-bee-hive [last accessed 12 May 2015].
2   Kirsten Bradley, 'Is the flow hive a good idea?', *Milkwood*, 26 February 2015. http://www.milkwood.net/2015/02/26/going-flow-flow-hive-actually-good-idea/ [last accessed 12 May 2015].

it is part of a super-organism within which the comb functions as a central organ. The hive is the bees' home and supports their chemically enabled communication system. The replacement of an adaptive wax hive by a rigid man-made plastic one creates a functionally depleted and sometimes toxic environment. The imposition of standardized cells prevents the bees from breeding drones throughout the hive; this reduces genetic diversity among surrounding bee populations, and resilience is reduced. Instead of thinking of the colony as a complex living system, the inventors of Flow Hive imagine insects as components of a production machine in which they are manipulated to suit the human desire for profit and efficiency.

Flow Hive is just one example among myriad human inventions of a design approach that impedes interconnectedness between the elements and the whole in healthy living systems. In a perpetual search for order and control, we privilege the abstract over the lived and impose idealized solutions that are at odds with how healthy living systems actually behave. We strive for perfect, static, utopian solutions that are different, in kind, from real-world ecologies, which are dynamic and constantly changing. This habit of mind is not limited to the engineering of hard systems; some visions of nature itself have been utopian in this sense. Until recently, conservation research tended to focus on the individual species as the unit of study—for example, by looking at the impact of habitat destruction on an individual's situation. But there is now increasing recognition that species interactions may be much more important. As the ecologist Jane Memmott has explained, all organisms are linked to at least one other species in a variety of critical ways—for instance, as predators or prey, or as pollinators or seed dispersers—with the result that each species is embedded in a complex network of interactions.[3] The extinction of one species can lead to a cascade of secondary extinctions in ecological networks in ways that we are only just beginning to understand.

Since the 1980s, scientific discoveries have confirmed the proposition that no organism is truly autonomous. Researchers specializing in Gaia theory, systems thinking and resilience science have shown that our planet is a web of interdependent ecosystems; the dead, mechanical object that has shaped scientific thought for most of the modern age turns out to have been misguided. From the study of everything from sub-microscopic viruses, yeasts, ants, mosses, lichen, slime moulds and mycorrhizae, to trees, rivers and climate systems, a new story has emerged. All natural phenomena are not only connected: their very essence is to be in relationship

3   Jane Memmott et al., 'The Conservation Of Ecological Interactions', Centre for Functional Ecology, University of Coimbra, 2010. http://cfe.uc.pt/files/ memmott_et_al_2010_roy._entomolog._soc._the_conservation_of_ecological_interactions.pdf [last accessed 12 May 2015].

with other things—including us. On a molecular, atomic and viral level, humanity and 'the environment' literally merge with one another, forging biological alliances as a matter of course.

Although our culture does not equip us well to grasp these hidden connections, knowledge of their existence is literally vital. For thinkers such as the physicist Fritjof Capra, the greatest challenge of our time is to foster widespread awareness of the hidden connections among living—and non-living—things. In a powerful follow-up to Capra's challenge, Stephan Harding, in his book *Animate Earth*, describes how the world works not only on the macro level (the atmosphere, oceans or Earth's crust), but also on a micro level: plankton and bacteria contribute to the formation of clouds by acting as nuclei for water droplets; mycorrhizal fungi team up with plants that grow in poor soils; chemical signals called pheromones allow ant colonies to behave like a super-organism. Co-evolution—the formation of bio-cultural partnerships—turns out to be how our fertile planet thrives, says Harding; although we have ruptured these relationships, it is not too late to build bridges so that Earth can become healthy and self-regulating once again.[4]

These scientific findings resolve one question that has vexed philosophers more than any other: where does the mind end and the world begin? Until recently, we tended to think of the nervous system as a glorified set of message cables connecting the body to the brain—but from a scientific perspective the boundary between mind and world turns out to be a porous one. The human mind is hormonal as well as neural. Our thoughts and experiences are not limited to brain activity in the skull, nor are they enclosed by the skin. Our metabolism and nature's are interconnected on a molecular, atomic and viral level. Mental phenomena—our thoughts—emerge not merely from brain activity, but from what the philosopher Teed Rockwell has described as 'a single unified system embracing the nervous system, body, and environment'.[5] The importance of this new perspective is profound. If our minds are shaped by our physical environments and not just by synapses clicking away inside our box-like skulls, then the division between the thinking self and the natural world—a division that underpins the whole of modern thought—begins to dissolve. Having worked hard throughout the modern era to lift ourselves 'above' nature, we are now being told by modern science that man and nature are one after all.

4   Stephan Harding, *Animate Earth: Science, Intuition and Gaia* (Cambridge: Green Books, 2009).

5   Teed Rockwell, *Neither Brain nor Ghost: A Nondualist Alternative to the Mind-Brain Identity Theory*, (Cambridge, Mass.: Bradford Books, 2005).

Ecological networks also involve things. In today's world we are taught to perceive the things around us as lifeless, brute and inert. Nature, insofar as we think about it at all, is a nice place to go for a picnic. With this picture of the world in mind, we fill up our lives, lands and oceans with junk without a second thought. But we used to think quite differently: the idea that things might be 'vital' was first expounded formally by Greek philosophers known as hylozoists, or 'those who think that matter is alive'; they made no distinction between animate and inanimate, spirit and matter. For Roman sages, likewise: in his epic work *On The Nature of Things*, the poet Lucretius argued that everything is connected, deep down, in a world of matter and energy. Ancient Chinese philosophers also believed that the ultimate reality of the world is intrinsically dynamic; in the *Tao*, everything in the universe, whether animate or inanimate, is embedded in the continuous flow and change. In Buddhist texts, images of 'stream' and 'flow' appear repeatedly; they evoke a universe that is in a state of impermanence and ceaseless movement. In 17th-century Europe, the Dutch philosopher Baruch Spinoza conceived of existence as a continuum, an inseparable tangle of body, mind, ideas and matter. And just seventy years ago, Maurice Merleau-Ponty was an advocate of not only being in the world, but also belonging to it, having a relationship with it, interacting with it, perceiving it in all dimensions.

The belief that matter matters, so to speak, was obscured by the fire and smoke of the thermo-industrial economy. Fossil fuels had powered economic growth so powerfully since the 19th century that we lost sight of the fact that this model might be of limited duration owing to constraints on resources. Now, as those constraints make themselves felt, many of these ideas are resurfacing. For thinkers in the 'new materialism' movement, our relationship with the material world would be more respectful, and joyful, if only we realized that we are part of the world of things, not separate from it. Timothy Morton, for example, is adamant that there is more to 'things' than we know in the 'vast, sprawling mesh of interconnection without a definite centre or edge' that constitutes our world.[6] Another philosopher, Jane Bennett—responding, in her words, to a 'call from our garbage'— advocates a patient, sensory attentiveness to what she calls the 'vibrancy' of matter and the nonhuman forces that operate outside and inside the human body. Our wasteful patterns of consumption

6    Timothy Morton, *Ecology without Nature: Rethinking Environmental Aesthetics* (Cambridge, Mass.: Harvard University Press, 2009).

would soon change, she reckons, if we saw, heard, smelled, tasted and felt all this litter, rubbish and trash as lively—not just inert stuff.[7] 'Sometimes those sticking their heads in the sand are looking for something deep,' quips yet another philosopher, Peter Gratton; when everything around is understood to be 'vital', he asks, what political and ethical consequences follow? Do bacteria count as life? Viruses? A robot? Is the ecosystem itself a life? If the answer to any of these questions is yes or even maybe, Gratton argues, then the assumption that we humans have a right to exploit the world to our own ends begins to break down.[8]

## HOW INNOVATION HAPPENS

In this context, change and innovation are no longer about finely crafted 'visions' and the promise of a better reality described in some grand design for some future place and time. Change is more likely to happen when people reconnect—with each other, and with the biosphere—in rich, real-world contexts. This proposal may well strike some readers as being naive and unrealistic. But, given what we now know about the ways complex systems—including belief systems—change, my confidence in the power of the Small to shape the Big remains undimmed. We have learned from systems thinking that profound transformation can unfold quietly as a variety of changes and interventions, and often small disruptions accumulate across time. At a certain moment—which is impossible to predict—a tipping point or phase shift is reached, and the system as a whole transforms. It is a lesson confirmed repeatedly by history: 'All the great transformations have been unthinkable until they actually came to pass,' writes the French philosopher Edgar Morin: 'the fact that a belief system is deeply rooted does not mean it cannot change.'[9]

The eco-philosopher Joanna Macy describes the appearance of this new story as 'The Great Turning': a profound shift in our perception, and a reawakening to the fact that we are not separate or apart from plants, animals, air, water and the soil.[10] There is a spiritual dimension to this story (Macy is a Buddhist scholar), but her 'Great Turning' is consistent with recent scientific discoveries, too: the idea, as articulated by Stephan Harding, that the world is 'far more animate than we ever dared suppose'. Explained in this way—by science, as much as by poetry, art and philosophy—the

7   Jane Bennett, *Vibrant Matter: A Political Ecology of Things* (Durham, N.C.: Duke University Press, 2010).

8   Peter Gratton, 'Vitalism and Life', *Philosophy in a Time of Error*, 15 June 2010. http://philosophyinatimeoferror. com/2010/06/15/vitalism-and-life/ [last accessed 12 May 2015].

9   Edgar Morin, *Homeland Earth: A Manifesto for the New Millennium* (New York: Hampton Press, 1999).

10  Joanna Macy, 'The Great Turning'. http://www.joannamacy.net/ thegreatturning.html [last accessed 12 May 2015].

earth no longer appears to us as a repository of inert resources. On the contrary: the interdependence between healthy soils, living systems and the ways we can help them regenerate finally addresses the 'why' of economic activity that we have been lacking.

This new story does not negate the value of a proactive and systematic approach to design, but it does mean paying at least as much attention to the connections and interactions *between* elements of a system as to discrete components. As we saw with the Flow Hive, the danger in a product-only approach is that it imposes a too rigid framework on a situation in which a community—such as the bee colony, a super-organism—needs constantly to change if it is to remain healthy and resilient. A growing worldwide movement is looking at the man-made world through a fresh lens. Sensible to the value of natural and social ecologies, it is searching for ways to preserve, oversee and restore assets that already exist (so-called 'net present assets') rather than think first about extracting raw materials to make new components from scratch. Designers and manufacturers have an important contribution to make in this movement. Designers can very usefully cast fresh and respectful eyes on a situation to reveal material and cultural qualities that might not be obvious to those who live in them. This kind of regenerative design reimagines the built world not as a landscape of frozen objects, but as a complex of interacting, co-dependent ecologies.

# THOMAS LOMMÉE

# AN OPEN INVITATION TO THE GRID

# An Open Invitation to the Grid

## Interview with Thomas Lommée

INTERVIEWER   Can you imagine a system that is finished or in a complete state? Is there any system that is …

THOMAS LOMMÉE   … that's completely worked out? I don't think so. A system is always a type of methodology, a framework within which things happen—a filter through which things pass. It's always in movement. I don't think a system can be finished.

In your OpenStructures project, you're exploring this idea of the constantly evolving system by using a shared design grid that allows multiple partners to contribute parts, components and structures to a single project. How does that affect the design process?

TL   What's being proposed in the OpenStructures project is a kind of shared design framework. That, of course, introduces certain restrictions: as a designer you no longer have total design freedom. But by sticking to shared rules, new opportunities are enabled, so what you design will be able to communicate with what other people are designing and creating. This will create new opportunities for re-use and new incentives for disassembly, and it will stimulate people to build further on each others' designs, thus creating an environment in which collaboration feels more natural: what my competitor is designing might also be useful for me, and vice versa. The goal is to create a system that distributes the wealth it generates. The idea is that, as an individual, you no longer have to imagine the whole system. You can just add to what has already been done by others.

This project is very much about modularity. What made you choose the term 'structure' instead of 'system'?

TL   An open system can be an open transportation system or an open knowledge system, so I thought it was important to have the word 'structure' in there to indicate that it relates to buildings and objects, to tangible things. The term 'structure' could refer to a tent or scaffolding, but it could also be a kitchen appliance or other small-scale structure. I wanted to have a term that would encompass differences of scale.

'OpenStructures (OS) Relatives' project designed by Thomas Lommée's masterclass, alongside existing components contributed by other designers, installation view, Milan, 2015

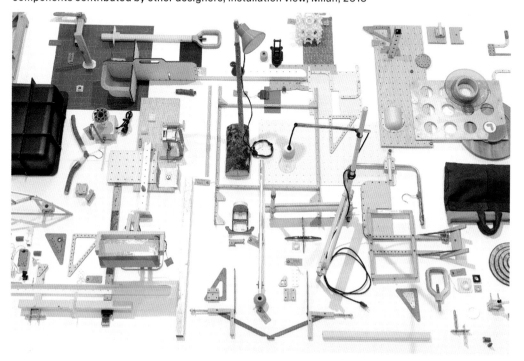

What is it that makes single parts form a system?
Does there need to be an interface?

TL   What I'm starting to see is the development
of different families that all have their own interface,
and that are all clustered around one interface.
Within the same system you also have a lot of parts
that don't work together. It's not that everything
fits with everything else. Actually, that's impossible,
and perhaps also not desirable. Certain parts are
popular and evolving, and other parts just kind of
slowly die because nothing happens with them or
they are not found to be interesting enough.

Do you refer to existing systems when developing
something like OpenStructures?

TL   I try to refer as much as possible to existing
systems. Before arriving at a grid of 4 × 4 cm,
I measured everything I could find for six months

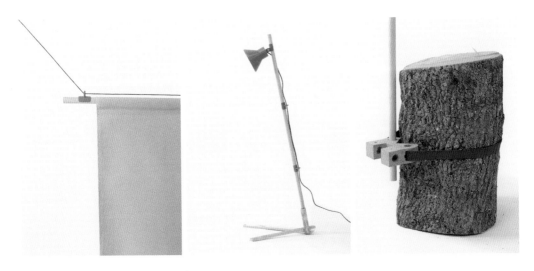

in order to identify common denominators. First,
because if they exist, it means they make sense:
they're used by a lot of people, so they just work.
Second, because then it's easier to build on what
already exists. You can see modularity and
collaborative systems in language, in that it's also
a kind of open standard, a shared framework that
enables different people to communicate and to
collaborate. The larger your field of collaboration
becomes, the greater the need to have a kind of

↑ 'OpenStructures (OS)
Relatives' from Thomas
Lommée's masterclass, 2014–15

→ The masterclass's
presentation at the Domaine
de Boisbuchet, France, 2014

Presentation by Thomas Lommée's masterclass at the Domaine de Boisbuchet, France, 2014

shared communication framework. That's what you see with English as it spreads everywhere. It's the same with standards. Look at when container ships were invented. They just emerged out of a shared need for a more efficient logistical framework that worked for everybody involved in that system. The same applies all the way down to beer crates and maybe sugar cubes. Perhaps there is a relationship between the size of a sugar cube and the dimensions of a container ship, because they're like Russian dolls, with one fitting into another.

Does this kind of logic belong to a certain epoch?

TL    I do think that this approach is a logical consequence of a networked society. You started to notice it with open-source software. Things usually happen first in a digital context, because you don't have the material aspect: you just copy and paste without losing any material or incurring costs. Now it's started to appear in hardware. You begin to see similar initiatives all over. That indicates there's a pattern, that it's a logical consequence. Where each initiative will lead, or how successful it will be, is hard to predict.

Is this kind of design the strategy of the future?

TL    No, it's still an open question. It's an interesting process for sure, and it makes you look differently at things. As a designer, you're trained to be very judgemental. You either like something or you don't; you think it's beautiful, or you think it's ugly. In this context the choice is no longer relevant, because you rather start to imagine what it could become, which parts could be interesting to use, how you could reconfigure it, who else could use this or that part, and so on. The discussions that emerge around this topic are completely different from discussions about aesthetics; I'm happy not to have those kinds of discussions anymore. We noticed this during the USM masterclass, where participants used the OpenStructures grid to develop an object of which at least one part was used in the design of a fellow student, or an object that could even be combined with organic material: a tree branch, for instance, that might become a lampstand connecting with an OpenStructures part. Whether you liked the other participant's design wasn't important; you had to find a way to use it. I think that's the essence of open design: that you no longer assume that you've found the truth. Is it a solution for the larger problems we're faced with? It's difficult to say, because nothing whatsoever is in production. It's all at the stage of prototypes and workshops.

How do you see OpenStructures functioning as an economic model? What is the benefit for designers who contribute to your system, who are willing to work within your framework?

TL    At OpenStructures we're asking a lot of people to give up their design freedom and to try to work within certain parameters. But the research is now very much around what you open and what you close within that framework. What if you have an object that has been initiated by one person, improved by another one and then again by somebody else? What if you want to sell that product? How does that work? How do you divide the profit? Do you protect

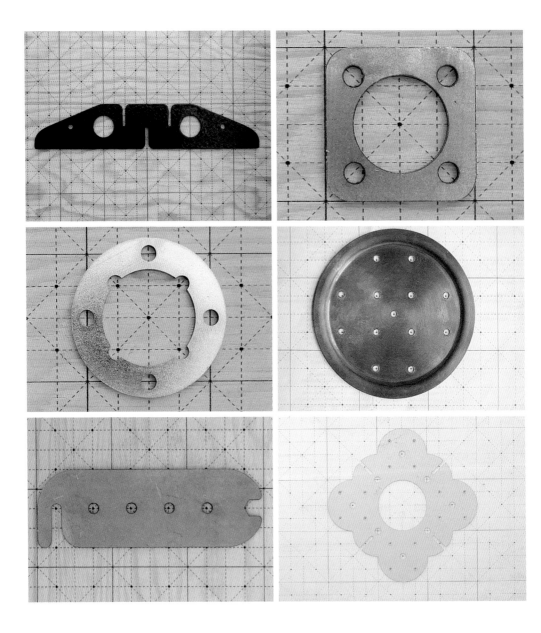

Lukas Wegwerth, 'OpenStructures
Part SCA_15', 2013

Lukas Wegwerth, 'OpenStructures
Part SCA_31', 2013

Lukas Wegwerth, 'OpenStructures
Part SCA_30', 2013

Lukas Wegwerth, 'OpenStructures
Part SCA_32', 2013

Kirstie Van Noort, 'OpenStructures Part for
Cooking Set', 2009–2010

Fabio Lorefice, 'OpenStructures Part No. 051',
2009

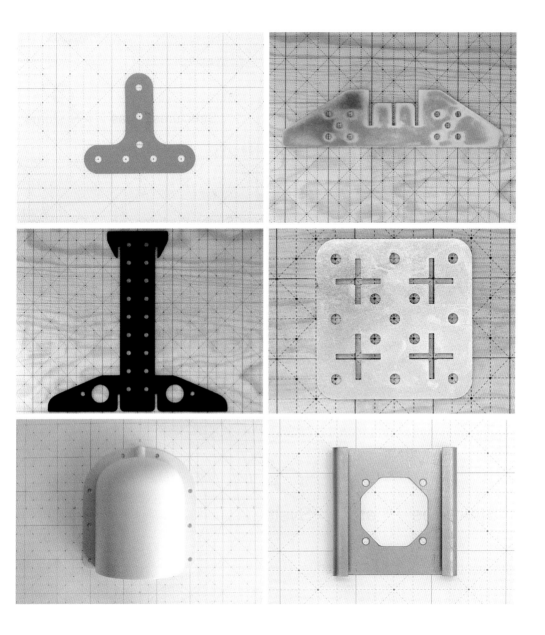

Fabio Lorefice, 'OpenStructures Part No. 047', 2009

Lukas Wegwerth, 'OpenStructures Part SCA_11', 2013

Marianne Cardon, 'OpenStructures Lamp Shade Part', 2015

Lukas Wegwerth, 'OpenStructures Part SCA_10', 2013

Lukas Wegwerth, 'OpenStructures Part SCA_18', 2013

Dries Verbruggen, 'OpenStructures Adaptor Piece', 2009

the designs or do you leave them open? How do you make something in such a way that people who contributed to it feel that they're recognized for the work they did? That's where I am at this point. The ecological benefits are clear: you facilitate re-use, and objects become more resilient because they can adapt to their context. I think the social benefit is clear, because it creates a more collaborative environment and new social spaces where people can gather, take things apart and build further. I can see this aspect working. As far as the economics are concerned, that's still the question that needs most thought and most development. How do you create an economical model that distributes wealth and creates a win-win situation for everybody? If that element isn't figured out, the whole project will remain a design experiment.

I would like to come back to the question of aesthetics. You mentioned that you were glad to have finished discussing aesthetics and design, but you are showing pieces of OpenStructures within an exhibition context as well, including the 'rethink the modular' exhibition in Milan. To be honest, I'm pretty sure that you are concerned with the aesthetics of the examples on display. Do you think that modules need to be exhibited in such a way that people can perceive them as part of a modular system?

TL    I think we have no choice. The grid should be seen as a three-dimensional script that generates certain objects. This script generates a certain kind of aesthetic and a certain kind of object. It's just the nature of the system. You should work with it, and you should acknowledge that this is its aesthetic. This is a niche approach, and it might appeal only to a certain type of person who shares the value set that is behind the system, because every aesthetic actually materializes a certain set of values. The values here are re-use, autonomy, self-repair, adaptation and collaborative modes of construction. I think the project is as big or as small as the community that is willing to embrace it. There is also a negative connotation with regard to modular systems. They can appear very totalitarian very quickly, but I also think that's because such systems were very frequently initiated from the top down. It was often governments that built complete modular living units or neighbourhoods. We know that this doesn't work. I hope that, by opening up and decentralizing modular systems, different signatures will be combined and thus more diversity will develop within each system.

Could you conceive a non-modular environment or non-modular design?

TL    Of course! From my point of view it's good that you have both modular and non-modular designs. In modularity's most successful form, maybe fewer than one per cent of all things will be modular. What I've come to realize is that it works well within certain contexts, with objects that need flexibility because they evolve over time—like children's toys, for instance, where the child is growing and it's interesting to see if the object can grow at the same rate. Modular designs are more about the cyclical consumption of objects, about working differently with your built environment. In my point of view they have little to do with hyper-efficiency—there they lose out. It's as simple as that. There's no point trying to compete on that level, and we should just acknowledge it. Imagine a modular Ferrari—it just doesn't make sense.

Thomas Lommée, a tutor of one of the seven USM masterclasses, was interviewed during the 'rethink the modular' workshop at the Domaine de Boisbuchet, France, 2014.

# NATHALIE DU PASQUIER

# CATHARINE ROSSI

# THERE IS ALWAYS AN ALTERNATIVE

# ANTONIO SCARPONI

# JERSZY SEYMOUR

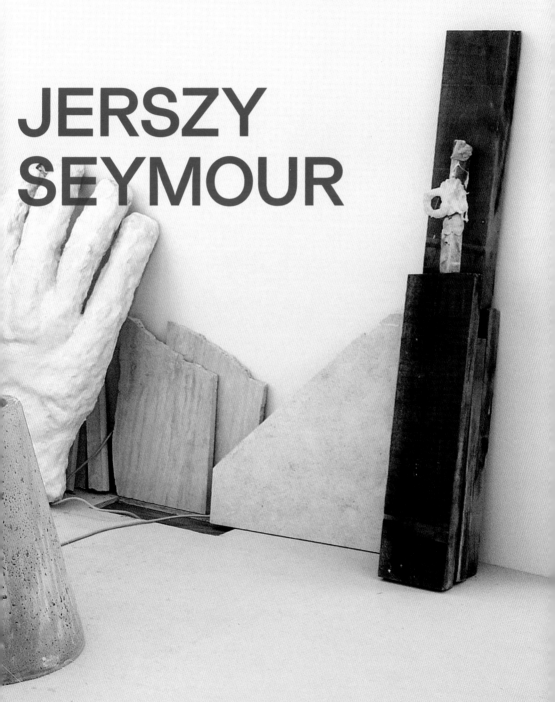

# There is Always an Alternative:
# Systems and Production

**Nathalie du Pasquier**
**Catharine Rossi**
**Antonio Scarponi**
**Jerszy Seymour**

CATHARINE ROSSI   Before we start to talk about alternatives, we need to ask whether there is still a kind of mainstream design activity that requires an alternative. Everything's quite diverse these days. The mainstream is fragmenting in different ways, but the idea of an alternative is somehow persistent. I think the idea that 'There is no one truth' is ingrained in real modular systems. I'd like to discuss how and why you have been interested in searching for alternatives in your work, in terms of production, working methods or materials.

NATHALIE DU PASQUIER   I started working as a designer in 1980, and I designed many textiles. Certainly these textiles are structures related to the idea of the module. I've recently started designing patterns for textiles once more. Of course, now I design from a different starting point because I have not done it for many years. But what I am more interested in now is the construction of space and objects that serve as models for my paintings and drawings. I am a painter, but I build sets. My constructions create relationships between volumes and spaces—pretty much like what happens in architecture, but on another scale. To answer your question more precisely, I chose painting as an alternative because it gives me complete responsibility for what I do.

CR   Do you think that having worked first as a designer influenced your approach when you turned to painting?

NP   I really wanted to get away completely from the design world. In fact, my first paintings were not even representational. I wanted a new way of life. But the other reason I decided to quit the design world was that I had the feeling we are surrounded by so many things—so many designers, so many industries. Instead I have become interested in using existing materials for my work, looking at existing objects and building things from existing objects. If you want to find an alternative way of life, you don't know where it will lead you. Of course, art does not replace products and buildings. But products and buildings can be looked at in a different, more poetic way. And yes, I think that, in the work that I have created over the last twelve years, I have allowed the designer in me to surface once more and to participate in the construction of my 'still-lifes'.

CR   What role does design have in connecting the mainstream— if it exists—with the creation of alternatives?

ANTONIO SCARPONI   As I understand it, design is a discipline that creates new relations between people and things. In this respect, it is a discipline that, almost by definition, is looking for alternatives. Somehow is it a discipline that explores, resolves and re-creates every time, every day.

CR   So what does being 'alternative' mean in terms of your work?

AS   I'm trying to find my own alternatives. It's a question of trial and error. It's a form of research that results in practical things and sometimes very impractical, very expensive experiments. But I'm trying to make them sustainable in the end. One way to do this is to reach a larger public, which is why I am experimenting with crowdfunding and making manuals that enable the consumer to recycle, divert and reconfigure existing products and materials against the backdrop of sustainability. The project that I'd like to mention here is what I define as an 'anti-product'. Anti-products are objects that are not supposed to be consumed, but they are supposed to be produced. In a way, they are devices that allow you to consume less. Let me give you an example: GQ, a fashion magazine, called me and said, 'Look, we have a sweater from Nike. They claim it costs 400 Euros, and we don't know what to do with it. We don't know how to feature it.' So my idea was to turn the hooded sweater, since it was really expensive, into five different objects that at any time could revert back to just being a sweater. The project is called 'Just Undo It'. It's a set of instructions on how to turn a simple hoody or a sweater into a computer sleeve, a back pack or a strap bag, with the idea that we don't need a new object. We need to learn how to transform what we already have. So the idea of design here is a form of knowledge.

CR   The idea of the alternative seems to underpin your design practice, particularly when it comes to working against existing cultures of production, distribution and consumption.

AS   I think that design is that kind of knowledge, and I also think that it goes far beyond the concepts of production or distribution systems. It may involve using a company's customer relations policy for alternative models of use and consumption. When I was invited to design an exhibition at the Cabaret Voltaire in Zurich (the birthplace of the Dada movement) about a revolution to smash global capitalism, my proposal was to smash capitalism with capitalism. So we built the whole exhibition using plastic boxes that came from Ikea. We fixed them together with zip ties, and the whole exhibition included bookshelves, a bed, tables and other features. We had a deal that, three months after the exhibition had finished, we would take those pieces back to Ikea and tell them we didn't need them anymore, in accordance with their returns policy. In this way the exhibition could travel more or less for free, and all we would need for the next venue was an instruction manual. It was the cheapest exhibition I ever built. I thought, what if I design something extremely simple and hack not only Ikea furniture, but also the company, using them as a distributor by relying on their infrastructure and their network? I introduced information that made it possible to subvert their system.

CR   Hacking, a term that has taken on different meanings over time, seems to describe your approach for dealing with the existing mainstream system.

AS   What we call 'hacking' is the most efficient way to understand the principles that regulate any system. If you know how the system works, you can hack it and you can subvert it. In this respect it assumes slightly different meanings in different historic contexts, but in the end it's the very essence of the practice we call design— a discipline that repositions the relationship between people and things every day.

JERSZY SEYMOUR   Stealing things from sweet shops to support the poor would definitely be satisfying, but it still constitutes a reaction to an unsupportable system. I am for a fairer and more equal social contract, and I think it's important to say it clearly: sweet shops will continue to be a problem! In my view the

Nathalie du Pasquier with Ajumi Han, napkin holders launched by Bodum in 1987

Nathalie du Pasquier, 'Kit N°2', 2014–15

challenge is how to find a way beyond the notion that an alternative current is simply a parallel of a mainstream system that I do not want do support. I have developed an alternative way to live, produce and consume by introducing the figure of the 'amateur' as an opposite of the 'professional' in my work. The series of works that belong to my conception of the 'Amateur Society' focus on the 'amateur' and his or her existential interests. The exhibition of 'The First Supper' at the Museum of Applied Arts in Vienna in 2008 was the first time that this idea of the Amateur Society was discussed with a broader public.

It took the form of an installation made from a wax material that could be melted down and used to connect other pieces of material. I talk about the material as a metaphor—as a connection between people, things and ideas. This substance can be melted and re-melted, a transformable material to satisfy changeable desires. The installation itself was set up over five days, and a kitchen in the corner supplied everything it needed. Furniture was also produced, and people were invited to a supper. At the end, everything was melted down for the next installation, called 'Salon des Amateurs'.

CR  In your work we find all sorts of alternatives: amateur makers, who are often debased figures in comparison with professionals; your conceptualization of material as metaphor; and your use of exhibitions as sites of participatory production rather than just the presentation of works to passive audiences. Can you say more about this combination of material, making and public authorship?

JS  The final part of three exhibitions based on the idea of the amateur was called 'Coalition of Amateurs'. On this occasion, materials were on hand so that the public could build things. In a way, that was the workshop part of the series. The idea was to break down a very theoretical idea of the Amateur Society into a whole programme of discussions. At some point the project had to be transformed. As it was, one product had been developed in 2009: the 'Workshop Chair', wooden slats held together by the wax material I mentioned earlier. So, talking all the time about an alternative society and finally starting to sell a chair, I asked myself: 'What the hell are you doing that for?' Actually, the point was to make some money to fuel a rocket ship, which was my metaphor for a school. A couple of years later we founded the Dirty Art Department at the Sandberg Institute, which is part of the Rietveld Academy in Amsterdam. So in a way the amateur workshop is one step closer to becoming a reality. We have students applying from all over the world. They get together, they discuss, we fight things out with them and we hope to effect a transformation.

→ Antonio Scarponi,
'Harvesting Station', 1:4
model, 2012

↓ Antonio Scarponi,
'T(h)un', prototype, 2015

CR  Alternatives appear so frequently in your work. Is there something that you're consciously working against?

JS  Without trying to talk about an ideal society, there are definitely things that are possible. The discussion about how capitalism works can be connected to the idea of design—it means talking about the social. If the history of art since the French Revolution has been about showing our failures, design and architecture have been about showing our belief in a modern, technocratic future. Today there is no revolutionary call, such as 'Everybody is an artist', but the aim is that everybody should have the opportunity to cherish their actions as an art form, and this can extend to the wider context of society. Since the collapse of the 1960s art movements, the fall of the Berlin Wall and the critique of both modern and postmodern ideas, artistic positions that just reflect failure and design that expresses only success lose their relevance. The idea of 'dirty art' tries to embrace both poles of this discussion: it occupies a very precarious, schizophrenic position that requires poetry, humour and enjoyable human interaction in order to continue.

CR  Aside from designing chairs, furniture and everything that we see around us, should designers also envisage an alternative future society as part of their practice?

NP  We are responsible for our world, and we are responsible in every action that we take. In order to be alternative, you need to know what you are rejecting, even if you don't know where the alternative course might lead you.

AS  I agree. I suppose what we are trying to do is to build fragments of an ideal society by referring to a possible future. This is at least something I can relate to in my work, as a form of theoretical speculation. I suspect it probably wouldn't have any impact, but somehow it's a reflection that can be shared with other people.

CR  That concept of sharing and connecting brings us back to modularity and the idea of working with a system where everything is connected, be it through networks or ideas.

AS  In this respect, I think we need to move beyond modularity and beyond the idea of systems. It's about ecology, really—ecology in the extended sense of production, consumption, use and relationships. I think the act of design is a sort of lay prayer, a ritual, by which we come to an understanding about the world around us. In that sense, a new alternative, however small, is explored by designers everyday. And exploring an alternative is above all an imaginative act. An idea might be followed by practical actions that lead to an object, a product, a policy, and I guess this role in our society is given to 'the designer'. You can argue that design is an imaginative art—one that imagines tangible fragments of perfect worlds, of utopias—and that exploring 'the alternative' belongs to the act of creation. I believe this is part of a survival instinct that everyone has. To different degrees, the life of a product triggers an imaginative process that is shared between the designer, the manufacturer and the user. What I find interesting is that, today, these three roles can merge in one. And I would locate possible alternative models for design, production and consumption between these three roles.

js   We talk about modularity in almost the same way we consider Newtonian physics. Since we know about quantum physics, we know that Newtonian physics is very useful as an approximation, but it's not the one truth. In fact there would seem to be a multitude of truths, and, if we want to talk about communal ways of working together, we have to find flexible and open structures that support individual human experiences within a global society.

# RICK POYNOR

# THE
# PROSPECTS
# AND LIMITS OF
# CONNECTION

# The Prospects and Limits of Connection

## Rick Poynor

'Is there an ambition for a universal system that connects
everything with everything?' Wolf Mangelsdorf, a structural
engineer at BuroHappold, posed the question on the third day
of the 'rethink the modular' workshop,[1] and it was without doubt
the weightiest question to emerge from the week-long event.
The question is so large in its implications it was hardly surprising
that, at the end of the investigations by seven teams, it still hung in
the air as an unanswered challenge. No modular system conceived
to date aspires to a level of total modularity that can connect every
single element. We are not even close. To conceive such a system
would be to return to zero, start all over again and act like gods,
defining the possibilities and limits of every object within the
human-made universe of things.

Yet the ideal of total modularity is implicit in the very idea of
modularity. In a modular system everything is broken down into
separate components, and these components, the modules, must be
able to interchange with each other. For this to happen, there must
be well-defined interfaces that allow potentially limitless flexibility
of connection. By using modular components, manufacturers can

1    In order to discuss potential directions of     The 'rethink the modular' project invited
     modularity in architecture and design, a       seven teams from major design and archi-
     workshop was held at the Domaine de            tecture schools to the USM masterclasses.
     Boisbuchet, France, in September 2014.

reduce development time and effort. The standardization of elements means that manufacturing can be streamlined and consolidated, leading to potentially huge cost savings: different product lines employ the same modular design, and the prefabrication of elements makes assembly much easier. If some systems can benefit from working in an integrated way, then what might be gained in terms of efficiency and sustainability by even higher levels of modular integration?

We could start, perhaps, with the example of the smartphone, the most ubiquitous and defining new tool of our era. Dave Hakkens, a Dutch designer, has proposed an alternative smartphone design, known as 'Phonebloks', composed of modular components that look a bit like Lego. Hakkens argues that the phone would reduce electronic waste and save users money because it would be easy to upgrade as new features arrived. Each function would be assigned to its own separate replaceable module.

Dave Hakkens,
'Phonebloks' mobile phone
with add-ons, 2013

John Brownlee, a writer at Fastcompany magazine's online design section Co.Design, subjected the idea to systematic critique.[2] Smartphones, he argues, are integrated for a reason. In the iPhone 5S's A7 processor, CPU, graphics and RAM are compressed into a 'sandwich-like wafer'. 'Breaking this trinity up to allow for modular upgrades wouldn't just make the device run slower,' he writes: 'it would make your iPhone consume more power and triple its physical footprint.' The phone would be bigger, slower and more expensive than existing smartphones. Furthermore, Brownlee contends, the Phonebloks' design, far from being simpler, is a more complex way to construct a smartphone. Endlessly taking the phone apart to upgrade it would increase the chance of breakage and electronic wastage, as well as the cost to the user. Phonebloks, Brownlee concludes, is therefore the opposite of what

2   http://www.fastcodesign.com/3017409/
    why-lego-design-principles-dont-work-on-
    smartphones [last accessed 4 November
    2015]

Presentation by the Bless masterclass at the Domaine de Boisbuchet, France, 2014

it appears to be. It appeals to 'the part of us that wants the universe to be neatly ordered and precisely aligned'. The components organized on a rectangular grid are intriguing as design, but the concept does not add up as a piece of engineering.

For some participants in 'rethink the modular', the process of re-examination led rapidly to a questioning of the very notion of modularity. 'We avoid the word "module",' said the students in the masterclass led by the German fashion designers Bless. They were standing in the Japanese guesthouse that was their base at the Domaine de Boisbuchet, the location in France where the workshop was taking place. There was some irony in this statement, because the house was a beautiful example of early modular thinking, and occupying it for several days would have a powerful effect on the group.

Later, Desiree Heiss and Ines Kaag of Bless confirmed that they would never employ the word 'modular', which they felt to be overused, like 'sustainability'. They preferred not to work with a given theme and wanted to respond to whatever ideas the students put on the table. It was up to the masterclass to discover what was relevant, and it wasn't necessary that the outcome should please Heiss and Kaag as team leaders. From the group discussions, the idea of 'productive monotony' emerged, and they went on to explore the principle using repetitive actions designed to clear the mind. The team set out what they perceived to be the 'parameters of the good life' in a manifesto-like text. Any consideration of modularity, if it is to be effective, needs to begin philosophically, with first principles. What exactly is this system trying to achieve? If we lack a clear sense of the essential parameters, how can we devise modular solutions that will serve society's needs at every level?

To an observer—and that was my position at 'rethink the modular'—the reluctance of Bless to address the premise of the

USM masterclass and produce overtly modular designs could seem perverse, although were they not alone in taking this line. Usefully, though, their disinclination served to highlight a key issue that arises with the idea of the modular system. Human beings feel a compulsion to express themselves as individuals, and the resistance of the Bless masterclass to the theme of modularity was, in the first instance, a defiant assertion of the members' individualism. Designed artefacts provide countless opportunities to express our sense of individuality. Depending on our personal priorities, we are able to demonstrate, through these choices, our personality, taste, social affiliations, status, attitude to life and level of wealth. In affluent societies, we have been schooled as consumers to explore the possibilities of consumerism to the full.

But modularity must inevitably entail some degree of standardization. The more encompassing the modular system becomes, the less scope for individual expression it seems likely to allow. At present levels of modularity, this is not a problem. A modular furniture system, for instance, will coexist in an interior with numerous non-modular elements that have no ability or ambition to connect with each other. I own a modular metal shelving system, and it does a fine job of quelling the chaos that might otherwise overwhelm my office. The pleasurable sense that my long-term commitment to this system says something positive about me (even though many people have the same product) comes from the contrast it forms with the rest of my non-modular possessions and furniture. I have no desire for everything to be ordered and precisely aligned.

Let us consider the printed book as a kind of module. That is how the 'rethink the modular' team led by Allan Wexler, an artist

Working model produced by Allan Wexler's masterclass, Domaine de Boisbuchet, France, 2014

and designer, approached the idea of the traditional codex. 'Can the module of the bound book balance the specificity of the unique content contained within its covers?' he asked. The most obvious form of modularity in books is internal and structural. Each page is a module shaped by an invisible geometric grid that determines where typographic and pictorial elements will fall, so as to achieve continuity and order throughout. A book may also have a modular relationship with other books through consistency of page size. A series of books produced by a publisher will all look and feel like modular expressions of a linking editorial idea. But books come in a huge variety of grids and physical sizes, and any two volumes compared at random are unlikely to have a modular relationship. Here, again, designers have tended to resist larger attempts at standardization, often preferring irregular page sizes to ISO international sizes.

The idea of a 'conceptual shelf' emerged early on from Wexler's masterclass, and the participants ended up building a store to house a collection of books. The wooden storage and seating units could be connected, via a grid of rods, to form a potentially endless modular reading platform limited only by the space available. Here, modularity became a metaphor representing the mental connection implicit in a community of readers.

Connection, although of a different kind, was also the theme of the industrial designer Dimitri Bähler's workshop. 'Modularity means, for me, interaction,' he says. The modularity in this case lies in the idea of a potentially expandable structure of disparate and non-modular, though still closely interconnected, elements. What

Presentation by Dimitri Bähler's masterclass at the Domaine de Boisbuchet, France, 2014

counts is the combined effect. Five machines—interactive electronic installations powered by programmable Arduino microcontrollers that had been elaborated by Bähler's team—formed a finely calibrated system in which each moving sculpture responded to inputs from other parts of the system and reacted with differing amounts of intensity depending on those inputs. As with the Wexler team's conceptual shelf, the final project was a poetic metaphor for the way that a system—here an interactive one—can be a great deal more than the sum of its component parts.

The team's machines were activated by breathing on a sensor. They looked interesting at rest, but their raison d'être was to perform a series of movements. Each section had a particular task—turning, climbing, swinging or inflating—with only a limited amount of programmable variability. In the near future, we will see modular machines capable of performing a wide range of useful actions. At MIT in the United States, researchers have built a self-assembling modular robot called M-Blocks. The modules, which look like building blocks from a construction set, can roll, jump, bond together and change their configuration to fit the needs of the task at hand.

The researchers wanted a simpler approach that required fewer actuators and moving parts, and would be easier to implement on a range of robots. Each module contains a brushless motor controller, a flywheel, a braking mechanism, electronics, a radio and a battery. A spinning mass in every cube means the robot does not have to be in a particular position to operate. Magnets in their faces and rotating magnets at their edges allow the modules to climb over each other, align themselves into new positions and snap together. The cubes can jump through the air, land on top of each other and reach places that would be inaccessible if they possessed only limited movement. They receive commands from a computer via a wireless link. In future, say the MIT researchers, the algorithms will be within the modules, which will be able to decide autonomously when, where and how to move. Human controllers will instruct the cubes to form a shape and let the swarm determine the best way to accomplish the task. In time, modular systems will be deployed in a wide range of construction and repair tasks. Self-assembling and reconfiguring modular furniture is another possible outcome.

The movements of these M-Blocks, which can be viewed online, are impressive to watch. The MIT project was not about the aesthetic dimension of modularity, yet even in its early stages it raised incidental questions about how extraordinary new kinds of functionality could be reconciled with the need for aesthetic appeal. This was a problem highlighted during 'rethink the modular' in the workshops run by Wolf Mangelsdorf and the industrial designer Thomas Lommée. As they both acknowledged, the standardization of modular systems reduces the possibility of differentiation between the elements and flexibility of form and expression. Visiting Lommée's masterclass in its temporary studio, Mangelsdorf observed that the design challenge was to 'not make the grid too obvious'. How do we reconcile the potential constraints of modularity with the natural human desire for aesthetic variety and individuality?

Lommée's project built on earlier research he had undertaken for the online OpenStructures modular construction project. The aim of his workshop was to create a system of everyday objects, one per student, in which each object—a fruit bowl, a lamp, a table, a hanging pocket for tools, a net and a hair dryer—was linked to the next by a common modular connector. The team's investigations showed that a family of products could reflect awareness that, even if we were some day to reach a modular utopia, much of the world would remain unmodularized. Accordingly, the team's system provided a point of interface between itself and the chaos of the world, and allowed an element of this chaos to enter the system— as with the coat hanger the students devised, fashioned from the branch of a tree.

It is hard to avoid concluding that, when it comes to the component parts of products, appliances and furniture, a high degree of modularity is unlikely to be possible without compromises in visual appearance that wrench objects away from the spectacularly smooth product semantics we now take for granted. Lommée told me during the workshops that he thought these compromises were inevitable in a modular system.

To fully embrace modularity in everyday product design, consumers would need to accept visual compromises as the basis of a progressive new aesthetic. We would have to learn to see sometimes slightly awkward modular components as signs of virtue, a means of conserving resources and using the environment wisely. This way of making and seeing things would need to become natural to us. No matter how flexible the system, in a modular utopia it seems unlikely that we could ever again permit the extreme degree of differentiation through design that we indulge in today because this amount of variety is so wasteful of resources. As beings driven by the need for status and a desire for variety and change, it remains unclear how we could transform such deeply ingrained expectations and remake ourselves along more rational lines. But if we imagine a distant future when we have achieved not just sustainability, but what the design philosopher Tony Fry calls a 'sustainment', then a very high degree of modularity seems essential.

What if we look to nature? Might we find fundamental principles of modularity in the natural world that can be applied to the artificial sphere? Lorenzo's Bini's team of architects had already

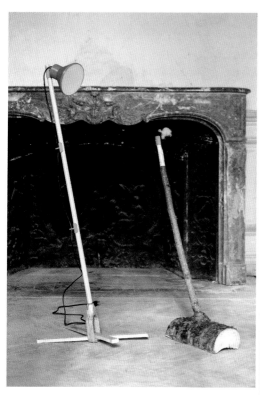

Three events at the Domaine de Boisbuchet, France, 2014:

← Presentation by Thomas Lommée's masterclass

↘ Presentation by Lorenzo Bini's masterclass

↙ Workshop meeting

done some preliminary work in Milan, looking at vegetation to discover principles of modularity, before they began the 'rethink the modular' workshop. They continued these explorations in the landscape surrounding the Domaine de Boisbuchet, collecting samples, making drawings and investigating such themes as functionality in trees; the geometry of tree growth; how trees generate their own joints; the relationship between a tree and its roots; the tree as a load-bearing structure and leaves as 'cladding'; whether there is a modular principle in natural colour; and the possibility of time expressed in modular form through the leaves' cycle of growth and decay. In the course of the week, the masterclass selected four themes to use as the basis of a series of 'monuments' dedicated to the ideal of modularity, all made from a single material: cork, card, wood and steel. Each monument was based on the serial repetition of a basic module. The pieces were not intended to have a function. They were freestanding experimental objects, close in appearance to abstract sculptures, designed to test the principles of modular construction on a convincing scale.

The MARS project, run by the Australian designer Alex Goad, is a modular artificial reef structure designed to correct the damage that human activity is causing to reefs in tropical and temperate waters around the world. 'Population growth, climate change, pollution, destructive fishing practices, increased water runoff and dredging are just some of the many contributing factors leading to the quick decline in our marine ecosystem's health,' writes Goad. The artificial reef, like the Phonebloks smartphone, is modelled on Lego principles. Ceramic modules fit together by means of connectors and tubular arms to form structures of varying sizes and configurations, depending on the characteristics of the sea floor. Each unit has natural-looking indentations that provide colonizing creatures with protection from predators, which cannot enter. The durable underwater structures act as building blocks to help repopulate damaged reef systems and allow the corals to grow back to their previous height more quickly. MARS shows that the contemporary imperative to rethink the modular is taking designers in the most surprising and productive directions. Goad's initiative achieves a perfect balance between structural innovation and restorative environmental intervention.

The natural environment proved a stimulus for more than one team. Indeed, nobody could have attended the workshop at the Domaine de Boisbuchet and not succumb to the beauty of the site, located deep in the French countryside. The teams of Lorenzo Bini and Bless developed project proposals in which the rural setting played a significant role either as object of research or source of programmatic inspiration. But no participants involved in 'rethink the modular' took it as far as the Japanese masterclass, led by the architect Go Hasegawa. They found staying at the Domaine de Boisbuchet to be such an absorbing experience that they wanted to discover an interpretation of modularity in the location itself. They did this by inscribing a mark on the land that was elemental in its return to first principles. Announcing that they wished to dig, they eschewed sophisticated planning and complex forms of construction, and set to work in the field outside the château where they met to discuss the project. Using pickaxes, spades and the energy of their own bodies, they excavated and flattened a broad hole, its depth determined by sitting inside it with their backs against the wall of earth. Their rationale was that, from this position, with their eyes aligned with the land, they would experience total connection with their surroundings. They had created their own crouching version of Le Corbusier's vertical Modulor.

It was a quixotic gesture, enacted with considerable good humour, which appeared, while it was unfolding, to be taking the masterclass in an unanticipated and perhaps unproductive direction. Yet the outcome had great presence. It is not often that anyone digs a hole in the ground for no practical purpose and proceeds to sit in it, and those who witnessed the precisely cut recess occupied by its makers felt its spirit. It was a lesson that any attempt to reconceive the modular has to start by accepting that human needs and desires must be reconciled with the organic world that sustains us and is our home.

# WOLF MANGELSDORF

# WE DON'T LIVE FOR A SYSTEM

# We Don't Live for a System:
# New Perspectives for Modular Architecture

## Interview with Wolf Mangelsdorf

I    INTERVIEWER   How has the vision of modularity changed over time—in particular since the modernist enthusiasm for suburban modular residential housing systems?

WOLF MANGELSDORF   The very fact that we're sitting here after a century of people thinking about modular design and how it should be defined just shows that it doesn't exist. In that sense we can only attempt to grasp the nature of something that might be a modular system or that has a particular raison d'être. I do think we need to question its nature all the time. I believe a shift has occurred. If you read Le Corbusier's theory of the 'Modulor', which derived from a certain understanding of the machine age in which industrial processes govern the world, it seems to propose a standardization of measurements, of processes, of room sizes—something that, in a way, has never worked. There was this idea of the perfect system where everything combined and worked together, from production processes to living environments. In my view it is a little too mechanical. A lot of those paradigms of industrial production have changed. There are emerging aspects of manufacturing that I think will completely alter how the industrial world works. What we've actually seen is that, with every little technological advance, be it in computer technology or in fabrication technology, things have become more individualized rather than more standardized, and there's a strong drive to make objects more distinct. I believe there was an inherent idea that, ultimately, it all fits into a system—a utopian kind of machine-age thinking—but it hasn't materialized. I think we've moved beyond that.

Do you invent a different support structure for every new project or do you reuse modular systems?

WM Both, I think. What we don't do is to have a geometric module that underlies the whole design. Yet modularity in design can be found throughout a project. The office buildings we design are usually based on a fit-out module. You don't see it, but the ceiling tiles and floor tiles all follow a 1.5-metre module. The grids are, wherever possible, multiples of these geometric modules. This is geometric modularity. Far too often we are still not thinking things through in that way, and architectural individuality overrides modular thinking. My quest here is to find that common ground where we can have a modular approach but still preserve enough design freedom and individuality so that we can customize our building.

How do you imagine creating that balance?

WM Individuality should happen on two levels. First, on a design level: my modular system should be versatile enough that, while I'm setting the design parameters and shaping my design, it still allows me enough flexibility to not produce the same building wherever I go, but to react to environmental criteria, site conditions, size and so on. Second, we should not standardize everything: users should not feel that they are in a modular building, and that if they don't sleep in a certain direction it doesn't work. We don't want to live like that either. That's a challenge. My first couple of years at architecture school I studied under Fritz Haller. That was my baptism of fire in modular design. If you look at Haller products,

↑ Moshe Safdie, Habitat 67, Montreal, 1967, construction photograph

← Habitat 67, view from ground level

→ Habitat 67, garden terrace in use

they're done to such a fantastic level of design, aesthetics and precision that they live in their own world. They're amazing, but they have all the hallmarks of what is actually problematic in modular design if you're not careful, because there is a risk that they have become standardized. The module governs your life, and that's not what should happen.

There is a tendency towards individualization, towards pluralism in design approaches. Would you say that, during the past thirty years of postmodernism, modules have become individualized within a system, or is that impossible? Do they have to be similar, or is that a modern notion?

WM   I'll use an example (maybe it's the wrong one). Consider façades: you can buy different versions from different manufacturers and eventually you can clad your building in any particular fashion, closed, open, with holes, fully glazed, whatever you want—but in fact every one of those manufacturers has already developed and applied their own systematic approach. And this systematic approach, this modular approach, governs their manufacture and how they are installed on site. Within that approach a lot of customization and individualization is possible, but ultimately we have just one choice of façade. You peel the topmost layers off and there's pretty much the same kind of thinking underneath each one.

We discussed Fritz Haller and his system, and you mentioned that he specified the size of gap that should exist between two modules—not because of how they connected, but because a certain amount of space was necessary.

WM   It's to do with the space between elements, the tolerance between individual elements and so on. It's all about how you put something together, because ultimately that's what it comes down to. We have pretty much mastered how to cast concrete. We have mastered how to cut steel, and the question is always how we should put the pieces together. A lot of thinking goes into those joins, and they have an impact on the whole. You can design the most beautiful structure and then destroy it just by not

Günter Behnisch and Partner/Frei Otto, Olympic Stadium, Munich, 1972

Richard Rogers in collaboration with Wolf Mangelsdorf/BuroHappold, Millennium Dome, London, 1999

→ Halle-Neustadt, Germany, kindergarten, 1966

↓ Aerial photograph of Halle-Neustadt, 1970s

considering the connections. Our thinking around modularity must now move from being about geometric modules to a systematic approach in conceptual terms and in the way it's put together. Here the computer plays a big role, because once you move beyond standardized production your logic slightly changes. At BuroHappold we come from a background of form-finding. Projects such as the Millennium Dome in London or the Diplomatic Club in Riyadh are all about form-finding and structure influencing the architecture. What I'm most interested in now is having other parameters, engineering parameters, come into that form-finding equation: solar performance, for instance, or the orientation of the building and considerations of shading and glare. All these aspects have a direct impact on the quality of a building, and they are really best addressed through form rather than technology. To put it simply, if I provide shade, I don't have to cool the building. The computer might help, but it might just result from a shift in thinking. It can be simple, but it's not always conducive to better architecture, because if the shading device does not form an integral part of the architecture or architectural expression, it becomes an add-on, an afterthought.

Your USM masterclass looked at how to develop a new system for largely modular buildings without the monotony of standardized living spaces that was common in municipal housing of the 1950s and 1970s. How are you trying to formulate and to apply a contemporary understanding of modularity in this context? Which architectural challenges are you tackling through the project?

WM We're not looking at the level of furniture or individual design components. We're looking at building design, and we are deliberately looking at residential buildings, because it is there we find the highest degree of complexity when it comes to the dichotomy between standardization and individualization. We're probably more tolerant in office environments, where we work with a 1.5-metre module. In our dwellings we may want to see things differently. We may want to change the bathroom every ten years and have it look different.

Life changes, and so do the homes around us—or they should. I chose that as a theme and, to make it challenging, I asked my team to look at multi-storey rather than single-storey buildings, where what you do on one level has a direct impact on what happens below and what happens above. That's where the challenge begins.

Do modules have to be legible to work together in a system?

WM   I don't think they do. It's something that should happen in the background, otherwise we run the risk that they will take over our lives, a bit like Superstudio: my table is all squares, the landscape is squares, and my building in the landscape is squares as well. I love that stuff, but it's highly theoretical in a sense. I don't want it to govern life. I think it should fade into the background. The thinking behind it should not actually shout 'modular' at you. There are instances where it exists but we never think about it. Think of your kitchen, your dishwasher: 600 mm wide. Your refrigerator: 600 mm wide. Your oven fits into the same module. The depth of your kitchen units is also 600 mm. Do you notice it in your kitchen? Does it govern your life there?

Yes, it does. It does constrain you, in so far as you have a limited space to cut your vegetables because in the next module there's the sink and the tap, and next to that there's the oven. So you have limited space in which to put your next module.

WM   Then your kitchen is too small! (*laughs*). If your building were modular, you could actually expand your kitchen. That's what I want to achieve here. To come back to your question of whether modularity should be visible, I think to a degree it will be visible, as far as it enables you to make changes easily or continue reshaping your environment in such a way that you don't have to get a jackhammer out or the demolition crew in. From that point of view, yes, it is visible, but not in the Superstudio way, where everywhere you look it's just a geometric module.

With Superstudio it was explicit. I mean, the table wasn't made from small bricks: it was actually a

Working model produced by Wolf Mangelsdorf's masterclass, 2014

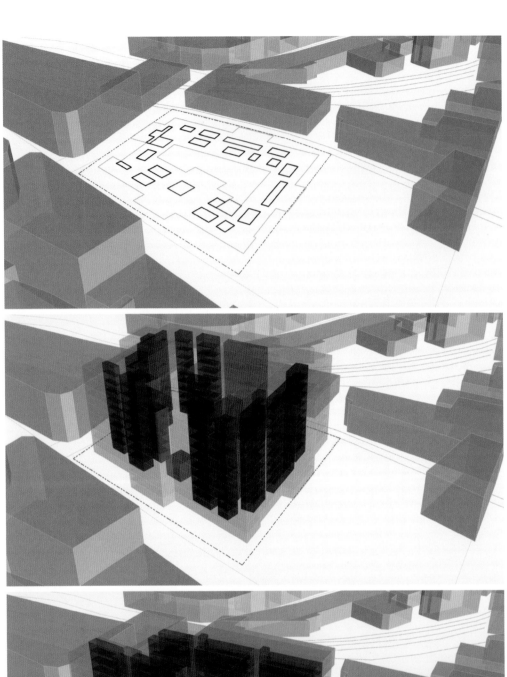

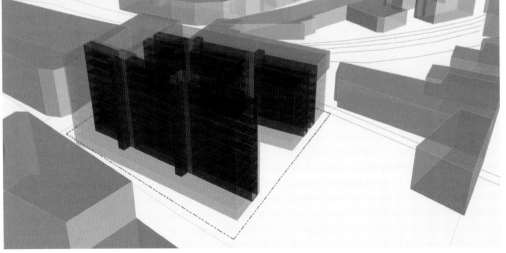

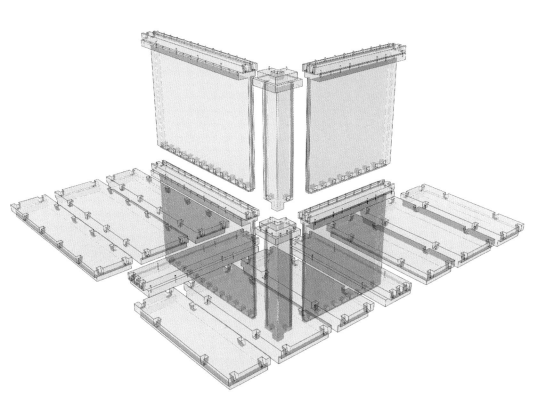

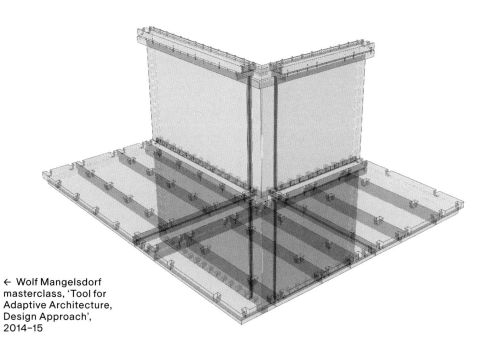

← Wolf Mangelsdorf
masterclass, 'Tool for
Adaptive Architecture,
Design Approach',
2014–15

↗ Wolf Mangelsdorf
masterclass, 'Tool for
Adaptive Architecture,
Kit of Parts', 2014–15

We Don't Live for a System    83

wooden table, and not even modular. It was more about making an idea visible, about the visionary utopian impact of that strategy for architecture.

WM    Absolutely.

Do you think these kinds of systems and modular ideas always have an author? Have they always been invented by somebody, or are they something natural that we seek out?

WM   Most of our buildings somehow work in modules. We like to set up a grid pattern, some kind of modularity. Very often it doesn't go beyond a dimensional rule that you use to design. We invent the module every time we do a building: we start afresh. We want to have the possibilities offered by a modular approach, but in the design process we also want an ability to configure things in such a way that the parameters still allow us some leeway. So we devise a geometrical module, for example, that can work in multiples. The ideal is that there should still be an element of individual configuration built in that allows you to play with the outcome rather than be locked into a standard result from the very beginning. That's the challenge. If I have a modular system that works on a dimensional module, I have a pretty much infinite number of permutations within given boundaries.

II

Since your masterclass, you've been developing a tool with your students that challenges the restrictions of standardization, adding flexibility and the possibility of reconfiguring elements within a given architectural framework.

WM   We looked at a design tool combined with a 'kit' of different parts. The parts are effectively the pieces with which we can build whatever we need to build, but the design tool allows you to introduce flexibility and individuality into your project. There are various levels of 'hardness' in a building: the hard parts are the ones that are there to stay. You hardly ever change a column, for instance. The core where you place your staircase usually remains untouched for fifty, maybe one hundred years, and there's not much need to change it if it's done well. Similarly, we defined as 'hard' those voids that you need to service a building, where you run your water, electricity and gas around the building. We then had a 'medium hard' category of elements: those that have a lifespan of, say, twenty to thirty years, where you place mechanical and electrical installations, water pipes, heating, cooling and ventilation. The façade of your building potentially also falls into this category. You also have the 'softer' elements that you might replace perhaps every ten years. You will change your kitchen because you get tired of your old one and want an upgrade. You change your bathroom because you want to reconfigure it.

> So the consumer or whoever makes use of the building has greater freedom to arrange the 'soft' parts?

WM   Absolutely. It gives the architect the freedom to design a building that possesses quite a lot of individuality. You're not fixed into one module: it's not all fixed dimensions. At the same time you have the flexibility to rearrange the softer parts within the building's hard frame during its lifespan. We come back to the idea that the logic of modularity does not revolve around always having the same parts. Instead, it's about connecting parts in the same way, and that is the sort of leap we tried to make. The logic of a system is condensed into its zones of connectivity—that's what we've concentrated on here.

Wolf Mangelsdorf, one of the tutors of seven USM masterclasses, was interviewed during the 'rethink the modular' workshop at the Domaine de Boisbuchet, France, 2014 (I), and on the occasion of the 'rethink the modular' exhibition in Milan, 2015 (II).

# GEORG VRACHLIOTIS

# HOW, THEN, DOES ONE ORGANIZE A CITY?

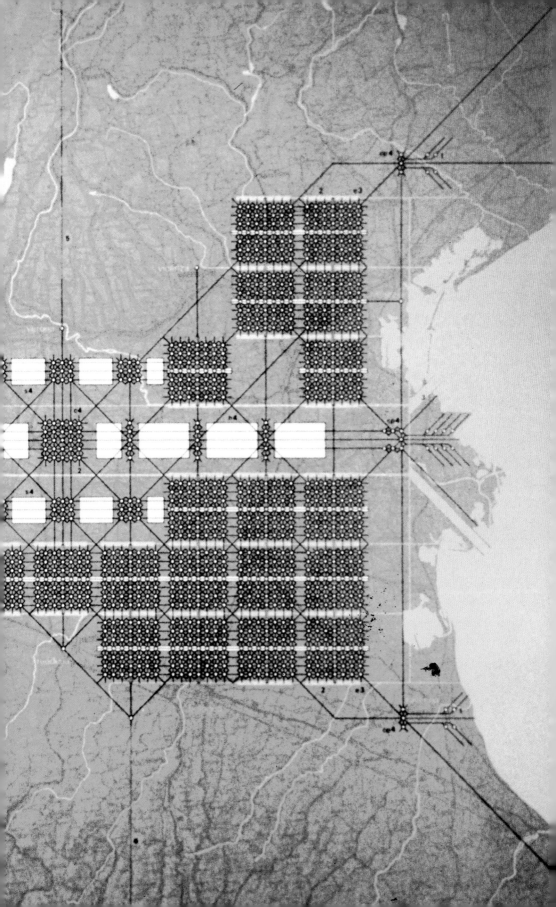

# How, Then, Does One Organize a City?
# Fritz Haller's City System

## Georg Vrachliotis

'Progressive anti-capitalist forces can more easily mobilize to leap
forward into global coordinations via urban networks that may
be hierarchical but not monocentric, corporatist but nevertheless
democratic, egalitarian and horizontal, systemically nested and
federated ... internally discordant and contested, but solidarious
against capitalist class power—and, above all, deeply engaged in
the struggle to undermine and eventually overthrow the power
of the capitalist laws of value on the world market to dictate the
social relations under which we work and live.'[1] This intellectual
argument for the importance of urban policy comes from David
Harvey's book *Rebel Cities: From the Right to the City to the Urban
Revolution* (2012), a polemic on the social role of the city in the
21st century. Harvey believes that the capitalist dynamics of boom
and bust are both reflected in the city, and his hypothesis is that
urbanization plays a decisive role in this. Cities are not only places
to live and work; they are also embodiments of political contexts.
Following on from the neo-Marxist theories of Lefebvre, Harvey
looks at what is known as the 'geographical imagination': the
image of society that is created by movement in and through space.
John Urry and Scott Lash believed that 'Modern society is a society

1   David Harvey, *Rebel Cities: From the Right
    to the City to the Urban Revolution* (London:
    Verso, 2012), p. 153.

on the move',[2] and Manuel Castells referred to it as the 'Space of Flows'.[3] Where Marx saw the reduction of working hours as the first step towards a decent life, Harvey points to the demand for adequate housing and acceptable living conditions for all. 'How, then, does one organize a city?' he asks, and thus puts his finger on one of the most controversial issues of the last century.

This question was also a matter of interest for Fritz Haller. Alongside other architects from the Solothurn region of Switzerland, including Alfons Barth, Franz Füeg, Max Schlup and Hans Zaugg, Haller has been recognized since the early 1950s as a leading figure of the so-called Solothurn School. As with many architects of his generation, Haller's approach to architecture was shaped by his personal experiences in the immediate post-war period: the sight of the unprecedented scale of urban destruction caused by the war, and the precision and aesthetics of buildings constructed in the US by European architects living in exile. It is no surprise that Haller soon came into contact with leading figures of the industrial building movement, who wanted to combine the aesthetic of Mies van der Rohe with the radical nature of automated building processes. This may have been one of the reasons why Haller accepted a commission in the early 1960s to design a factory building for USM at their production site in Münsingen, south of Bern. In order to fulfil his commission, he developed the USM Haller MAXI construction system: a modular steel-frame system that allowed single-storey halls to be built at a range of sizes. The structure was made up of columns and trusses that could be extended horizontally in any direction, as required—a particularly important consideration for an industrial building. USM were therefore able to plan further factory extensions as well as new administrative buildings. The MAXI system was followed by the development of two additional steel-frame construction systems: USM Haller MINI, a system for building on the scale of a two-storey family house; and USM Haller MIDI, a system for designing multi-storey buildings with integrated technology, in which the geometric arrangement of the service systems was treated in the same way as the geometric design of the building. In these designs, Haller wanted to explore 'the fundamental problems that any builder of complex modular systems must constantly deal with: geometrically arranging the system's modules, deciding how they should fit together, and ensuring that there is enough space to fit all the elements into their planned positions'.[4] Haller wanted not only to develop building

2   John Urry and Scott Lash, *Economies of Signs and Space* (London: Sage, 1994), p. 255.
3   Manuel Castells, *The Rise of the Network Society* (Hoboken, N.J.: John Wiley & Sons, 2nd edn 2009).
4   Fritz Haller, *bauen und forschen*, exhibition catalogue: Kunstmuseum Solothurn (1988), 3.3.0.

Fritz Haller, office building and production facilities for USM Headquarters, Münsingen, Switzerland, c. 1967

Fritz Haller, office building for USM Headquarters, Münsingen, Switzerland, 1965

↑ The USM Haller MINI system: Schärer House, Münsingen, Switzerland, 1969

→ USM production facilities, Münsingen, Switzerland, 1963

systems in a constructive way, but also to ensure that their spatial and temporal features could be geometrically classified and conceptually organized. His focus was on the development of a higher-level classification scheme whose abstraction was also reflected in its language. If we so wished, we could view this as a synchronization between a building system and a language system—a striking conceptual link that allowed Haller to interpret the city as a building system. It was therefore no coincidence that Haller increasingly began to deal with issues of infrastructure and communication on an urban scale.

The concept of what was previously understood as a 'system' in architecture was therefore radicalized and expanded in various ways. This radicalization was primarily reflected in Haller's two studies, *Totale Stadt—ein Modell* (*Integral Urban: A Model*, 1968) and *Totale Stadt—ein globales Modell* (*Integral Urban: A Global Model*, 1975). These works were not concerned with suggesting specific urban designs, but instead proposed graphic and geometric ideals that would require a comprehensive reorganization of the city. Even if Haller's above-mentioned quote is not interpreted as the formulation of a political idea, his writings make it clear that, as Harvey stated, there is no such thing as space that is entirely independent of social action. It is certainly no coincidence that a large portion of Haller's first study focused on the structure of the urban system—from the smallest unit, the so-called 'zero-order unit', consisting of a 'sleeping, resting and eating place for a family', up to 'fourth-order units', which could hold 61 million people. Each unit was itself made up of multiples of the next smallest unit. This therefore creates a nested urban system, whose conceptual framework resulted from a quest for a technically and geometrically optimized infrastructure. Using large-format diagrams with a striking degree of detail, Haller created an image of a technologically regulated future society, in which architectural objects dissolved amid the branches of endless networks. Like an enormous computer network, Haller began with individual nodes and expanded into a decentralized communications system that, owing to its high degree of abstraction, could be conceived only on a city-wide or even a global scale. The emphasis was no longer on the individuality and character of a space, but on its potential for integration into a smoothly functioning matrix.

The concept of infrastructure played a vital role in this. Haller saw infrastructure as an overarching cultural 'integration medium', whose significance extended far beyond its purely urban or functional meaning. Haller viewed the functioning of his ideal city in terms of geometry, rather like circular transport patterns. His precise drawings suggest that this geometrization of the environment would lead—particularly in West Germany—to a revival of the recently destroyed structures of the totalitarian state.

What resembled a slender antenna was in fact intended as a carefully calculated transport network for a city with many millions of inhabitants. The systematization of space, here carried to its extreme, turns out to involve an interplay of many different scales: construction nodes become traffic nodes and eventually communication nodes. The organization of a city was therefore understood as a collective project involving scholars of many kinds—'specialists in cybernetics, mathematics, electronics, physics, biology, geography, technology, psychology, sociology ...'.[5] For Haller, Norbert Wiener's cybernetic machine theory functioned as an avant-garde cultural code that could be used to describe a technological society of the future, within which architectonic objects dissolve into limitless networked systems. In *The Human Use of Human Beings*, Wiener famously declared that 'society can only be understood through a study of the messages and the communication facilities which belong to it'.[6] Correspondingly, at the centre of Haller's ideas lay not merely the theoretical considerations of architecture, but the development of model cities that—and here we see Haller's essential optimism about the future—support his claim that what the post-industrial world needed, against a backdrop of unchecked urban growth, was 'to create a meaningful environment for society'.[7]

Of course, Haller was not alone in this view. Many architects were beginning to work with concepts such as adaptivity, organization and control, in response to the widespread perception of a changing world of increasing technological growth. Eckhard Schulze-Fielitz's 'Space City' (1959), Yona Friedman's 'Spatial City' (1960) and Nicolas Schöffer's 'Cybernetic City' (1969) were early examples of this kind of thinking, and are representative of a whole range of utopian projects that envisaged humanity living inside enormous structures.

One particular project by Arata Isozaki, for example, clearly shows the extent to which people were caught up in the idea that the blurring of social spaces could be strictly regulated and controlled with technical models of thinking. The concept of the 'Computer-Aided City', as Isozaki's 1972 project was named, envisaged a huge urban system whose structure resembled an enormous aerial. A massive fibre-optic network, in which every receiver could also be a transmitter, would serve the city as an infrastructure system: 'If information is limited to one-way messages like television and radio, then the system is no different from cable TV. Since coaxial cables are able to transmit easily large volumes of information both

5   Fritz Haller, *Totale Stadt–ein Modell* (Olten: Walter-Verlag, 1968), p. 8.
6   Norbert Wiener, *The Human Use of Human Beings: Cybernetics and Society* (Boston, Mass.: Houghton Mifflin, 1954), p. 16.
7   Haller, *Totale Stadt–ein Modell*, p. 8.

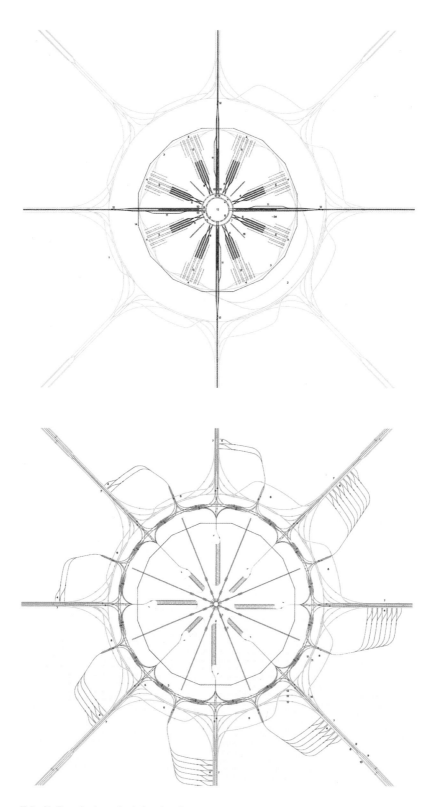

Fritz Haller, designs for infrastructure
and a public transport system for
*Integral Urban: A Global Model*, 1975

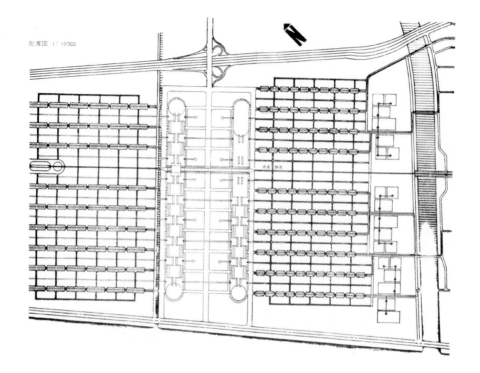

配置図 1:10000

ways, super-computers, if used to exchange, process and store information, can begin to serve as "the brain" of the city.'[8]

What sounds at first like a purely technical treatment of space turns out to be a concept for a city entirely controlled by machines. This was a radical idea, but it was also part of a broader movement. In his manifesto *Perspektiven einer Architektur*, Wolfgang Döring declared individual houses to be utterly irrelevant, stating: 'It is no longer a matter of individual things, of single isolated results, but of collective structures and networks that are receptive to future changes of a kind we may not yet be able to imagine.'[9] A system that can handle the unknown requires the greatest possible flexibility in its design, and the unknown in this case primarily consisted of 'continuous changes to our environment caused by communication media and technology'.

Both of Haller's books on the 'total city' are in no way inferior to these technological utopias. The dream was ultimately to find a way of spatially organizing social communication processes and thereby fulfil the utopian goal of providing technological systems for a supposedly more humane society. In the 1970s widespread predictions about world population growth also played a major role, first in evoking the threat of a society in disarray and, second, in seeking a way out through

8    Arata Isozaki, 'Computer-Aided City', in *Kenchiku Bunka*, no. 310 (1972).

9    Wolfgang Döring, *Perspektiven einer Architektur* (Frankfurt am Main: Suhrkamp, 1970), p. 13.

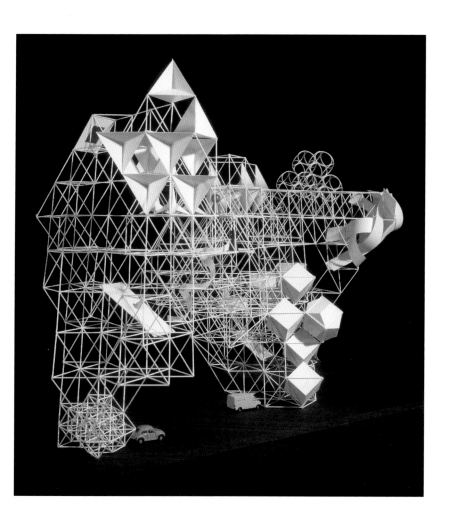

↖ Arata Isozaki, 'Computer-
Aided City', 1972

↑ Eckhard Schultze-Fielitz,
'Raumstadt', 1959

→ Fritz Haller, 'Study for
Problems of Connecting', 1968

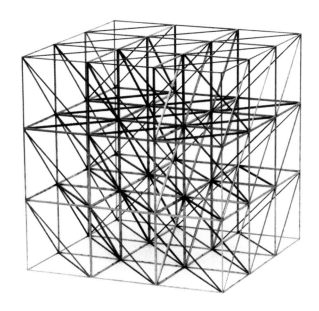

How, Then, Does One Organize a City?    97

LAST, BUT NOT LEAST, I GET BACK TO MY FAVORITE IDEA: THE "VILLE SPATIALE"

IT MEANS A PARTICULAR MIXTURE OF RULES AND IRREGULARITY

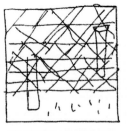

THE "VILLE SPATIALE" CONSISTS OF A MORE OR LESS REGULAR RIGID SUPPORTING GRID THE "INFRASTRUCTURE"

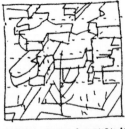

WITHIN WHICH INDIVIDUAL HOMES ARE INSERTED FORMING AN IRREGULAR PATTERN

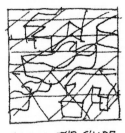

AS FOR THE SHAPE OF THOSE INDIVIDUAL HOMES ANYTHING GOES

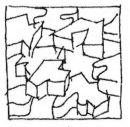

THUS THE "VILLE SPATIAL" IS A "MERZSTRUKTUR" AT URBAN SCALE FOR A MASS-SOCIETY CONSISTING OF INDIVIDUALISTS

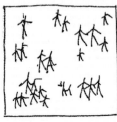

THIS IS OUR SOCIETY TODAY: A CROWD

I DO NOT KNOW HOW A "VILLE SPATIALE" WILL LOOK

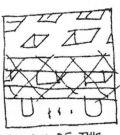

IT CAN BE THIS

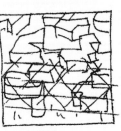

OR THIS

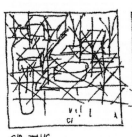

OR THIS

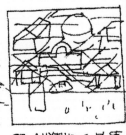

OR ANYTHING ELSE

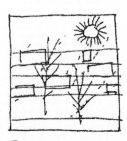

THERE IS NO GRAMMAR TO THE "VILLE SPATIALE" EXCEPT RESPECT OF DAY-LIGHT

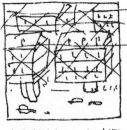

IT CAN LOOK AS WELL AS THE CITY YOU LIVE IN

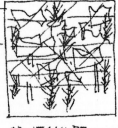

OR IT CAN BE COMPLETELY UNLIKE TO ANY CITY

IT CAN NOT BE PLANNED, IT CAN ONLY HAPPEN

Yona Friedman, 'Ville Spatiale', 1958–present

abstract systems that could be used to technologically control the world around us. Haller's core idea—which set him apart from other leading figures in this field—lay in combining the dynamics of social intimacy and community with the technical logic of industrial building. Another of his aims was nothing less than a systemization of the 'socializing function of space'.[10]

But suddenly it seemed that communication was not what we thought it was. Norbert Wiener's concept of communication as the invisible 'cement of society' was radically expanded in the ten years that followed Döring's manifesto. Alongside the popular image of communication as primarily a complex network of invisible relationships that no longer required any physical objects to exist, the image of a new kind of object came to the fore in the 1980s: the integrated circuit, better known as the microchip.

When the patent for the first commercially available integrated circuit was filed in 1959 by the engineer Robert Noyce, who went on to found the computer firm Intel, it launched an unprecedented quest for miniaturization in the fields of micro-electronics and silicon technology.[11] The technical potential for fitting large numbers of transistors, capacitors, inductors and resistors into the smallest possible space led to the creation of objects on an increasingly tiny scale, whose individual elements could barely be seen by the human eye. The technical structure of the microchip could even be described as an 'extremely concentrated form of the concept of networks that arose in the 19th century'.[12] The idea of being able to fit millions of transistors onto a wafer of silicon just a few millimetres square also sparked Haller's imagination. In an interview in the late 1990s, he explained the concept: 'Normal geometry is no longer enough to give us an understanding of the fusion between technology and culture. We need to find a language that can express these inter-connections. One example of this is the development of computer chips … If you look at a chip at a greatly enlarged size, it looks like a Mondrian painting. This is the new world. The structure of a chip is like the structure of a house. It's made up of horizontals, connected by verticals. Some chips include hundreds of layers on top of each other. Chips can no longer be grasped by our senses. We are alarmed and see them as inhuman. This is where the world really begins.'[13] Whatever Haller meant when he refers to 'normal geometry', it is clear that he was struck by the image of the

10   See Gernot Feldhusen, *Soziologie für Architekten: Wissenschaft in der Planungspraxis* (Stuttgart: Deutsche Verlags-Anstalt, 1975), p. 11.

11   See Leslie Berlin, *The Man Behind the Microchip: Robert Noyce and the Invention of Silicon Valley* (New York: Oxford University Press, 2005).

12   Martin Burckhardt, *Metamorphosen von Raum und Zeit: Eine Geschichte der Wahrnehmung* (Frankfurt am Main: Campus, 1994), p. 312.

13   Interview with Fritz Haller by Jürg Graser, 9 April 1998. See Jürg Graser, *Die Schule von Solothurn*, dissertation, ETH Zurich (no. 18051), 2008, II (Appendix).

← Engineers with an IBM 709 large-capacity computer at the CERN research centre, Geneva, 1970s

→ Piet Mondrian, *Broadway Boogie-Woogie*, 1942–43

↘ USM Haller, customized private bank interior, Nuremberg, 1986

enormously complex web of connections that are packed inside the minimal space of the microchip. It is pointless to speculate about the extent to which Haller truly believed in the analogy between architecture and microchips, but it is clear that many of the prototype designs and plans he developed in the 1980s include allusions to the structural aesthetic of microcircuits.

The fascination we feel when looking inside a circuit is not only visual, but also one of scale: it possesses an almost architectural effect. The delicate, complex grid of overlapping vertical and horizontal connections and the geometric arrangement of the wires are transformed by the eye of the beholder into an interplay between fiction and technology. Within the limitless world of the circuit, the microchip can be transformed into a network of cables, pipes, buildings or even an entire city. Haller was well aware of the associative potential and evocative power of these ideas. His allusion to the abstract paintings of Piet Mondrian also allows that artist's *Broadway Boogie-Woogie* (1942–43) to be viewed in a new light.

It may seem paradoxical, but the popularization of technology embodied in this image can be used to clarify the ideas on which Haller's identity as an architect was based. First, he held that concepts of space are epistemological models that are vital to the composition of society. Second, the subtle complexity of the spatial lies in its great imaginative potential; in this belief, Haller comes strikingly close to David Harvey's above-mentioned concept of 'geographical imagination'. Whether consciously or unconsciously, Haller was able to use the image of the microchip to gain insight into this field, but without losing sight of the practice of building. To him, the 'operative imagery'[14] of microchips was to an extent

14  Sybille Krämer, 'Operative Bildlichkeit: Von der "Grammatologie" zu einer "Diagrammatologie"? Reflexionen über erkennendes Sehen', in *Logik des Bildlichen:* *Zur Kritik der ikonischen Vernunft*, ed. Martina Hessler and Dieter Mersch (Bielefeld: Transcript, 2009), pp. 94–123.

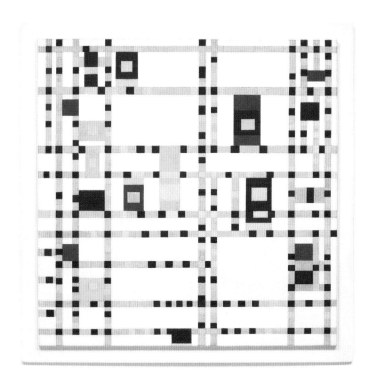

an idealized symbol of a description of conflict-free architecture as a technical system.

Today, almost fifty years later, we humans see ourselves as supposedly free agents with an ever-increasing range of available possibilities open to us. At first, it seems advantageous to keep our bonds as flexible as possible—a social strategy advertised with the keywords 'freedom' and 'networking', but whose façade may also hide the dangers of short-term thinking. Harvey calls this 'time–space compression and the postmodern condition'.[15] What is certain is that every step towards the networking of space could also be interpreted as a gain for 'symbolic world domination'. This seems to be one of the reasons why issues of logistics and infrastructure are attracting increasing attention in the fields of contemporary architecture and urban planning. Infrastructure networks demand social change: they affect the design of buildings, cities and landscapes, control the level of mobility available in urban environments, and set basic parameters for architectural and city planning.

The relevance of the term 'infrastructure' (literally 'the structure beneath') is that this is precisely what it seems to provide for architecture. The weakness of the term lies in the fact that it could all too easily be claimed to encompass the whole of reality, so that nothing remains outside it. If everything becomes infrastructure, it is no longer possible to adopt a standpoint from which architecture and the city can be viewed in a different way.

The issue of the meaning of urban spaces has long since ceased to arise only within the context of national and regional developments. In one way, Haller seems to have been correct: thinking about the principles behind a city—even when designing an entire city from top to bottom—always means tackling the question of technology from scratch. It also means delving deeply into the operational potential of infrastructure systems. Creating a convincing distinction between architecture and infrastructure, object and network, city and landscape becomes almost impossible when we are dealing with the potential and limits of an increasingly technologically modified environment. The new standard—and this is precisely what Haller wanted to introduce—means looking for connections that are global, although what we perceive may be heavily marked by European ideals. It may sound like a paradox, but Haller's ideal cities were nothing less than one of the most dazzling and radical attempts of the 20th century to use architecture to grasp the complexity of these relationships within post-industrial society. Haller made us aware of a new kind of technological restlessness—a restlessness highlighting the fact

15  David Harvey, 'Time–Space Compression and the Postmodern Condition', in *The Condition of Modernity: An Enquiry into the* *Origins of Cultural Change* (Oxford: Blackwell, 1989), p. 284.

J. Mayer H. Architects, 'A.Way', Audi Urban Future Award, 2010

that the fundamental issue regarding the future habitability of the digital world will be the difficulty of balancing the social complexity of the city with the intangible nature of technology. Dealing with this intangibility opens up unexpected realms of potential that not only include new ways of perceiving urban space, but also lay new foundations for exploring the built environment through models and simulations. Similar ideas were expressed by the architect Jürgen Mayer H. when he described his 2010 project 'A.Way', winner of the Audi Urban Future Award, as opening up new opportunities for the city through the digital networking of personal transport systems, allowing the urban future to be viewed as an exchange of virtual data streams through which personalized patterns of movement can be generated. It is as if humanity finds itself in an increasingly powerful socio-technological feedback loop between its real-world sphere of action and its digital equivalent.

Information technology is now taking over many more areas of life, but the idea of a city as a site for experimentation is nothing new. Zygmunt Bauman and David Lyon hit the nail on the head when they said that surveillance was not a new phenomenon but a 'key dimension of the modern world'.[16] The decisive factor in Jürgen Mayer H.'s project is not the design of a digital infrastructure, nor the evocation of a dystopian society of control, no matter how it is defined. It is much more about the design potential of interfaces in a system made up of people, objects and buildings. The focus is on the emergence of a self-sustaining hybrid culture, whose identity is made up of new cultural forms built around the encoding, recoding and transcoding of spaces, forms, surfaces and materials—a recursive process, in which intangible systems are adapted to fit physical systems and vice versa. The subject under discussion is nothing less than a new paradigm for urban spaces, in which faith in the power of geometric rigour has given way to the complexity of hybrid culture.

16  Zygmunt Bauman and David Lyon, *Liquid Surveillance* (Cambridge and Malden, Mass.: Polity Press, 2013).

# ALLAN WEXLER

# WORKING IRRATIONALLY WITH RATIONAL SYSTEM

# Working Irrationally with a Rational System

## Interview with Allan Wexler

I   INTERVIEWER   You are interested in exploring industrial standards in your work, often introducing them in an unusual or subversive way. How has modularity had an impact on your work over the past decades?

ALLAN WEXLER   Modularity has had an indirect influence on me. One great discovery was the work of John Cage, which is very much about setting up a system, a process, a set of rules. These rules and systems are in fact an abstract version of modularity. Those rules are really there to help the composer, artist or designer break through preconceptions of the way things should be done. A rational methodology is used to create irrationality. This is what advances culture and changes the status quo. That's what I'm interested in in my work. Some of the projects I created in the 1970s showed a lot of Cage's influence: I would make buildings and objects using predetermined quantities, dimensions, materials and time constraints, all of which allowed me to work in a subconscious and 'mindless' way. Later on, in a project called 'Crate House' (1990), commissioned

Allan Wexler's masterclass at work, Domaine de Boisbuchet, France, 2014

for the gallery of the University of Massachusetts
at Amherst, I worked using the crate as a module,
with its predetermined volume and the fact that,
in profile, it is the size of a standard American door.
In each crate, I provided the essentials for a bedroom,
a kitchen, a living room or a bathroom. Each of
those crates—as in Cage's work *Indeterminacy*—have
different requirements, different functions and
different furnishings. There is an idea of equality,
and within that equality there is difference.

> In works of yours like the Crate House, do you
> think that your modules have any relation to existing
> modular systems or structures, or did you invent
> them from scratch?

AW    I created Crate House in response to an
exhibition called *Home Rooms*. The University of
Massachusetts invited three architects to explore the
idea of home. Is there an underlying system? Yes:
much of my work revolves around standardized,
simple, almost banal kits of parts that can be found
in any lumberyard or DIY store. The module of

Allan Wexler,
'Crate House',
1990

4 feet × 8 feet [1.2 metres × 2.4 metres], which is a standard American plywood dimension, is a crucial one that I've worked with for many, many years. The 8-foot cube is a motif I have continually returned to, even in my most recent projects. Consider the idea of someone's home, which is so personalized and anti-modular, and yet squeezed into boxes. The interaction between the human body and these boxes is a source of irritation. The beautiful thing about systems and modularity is when you break the system, break the rules. But if you break the module too much, then it becomes boringly neutral. It's like a tile floor in a workshop: if all the tiles are laid in a Cartesian grid and one is slightly wrong, that one tile that goes against the grid is instantly recognizable. These breaks in system produce a shock, and that is what keeps us awake and alive.

> The students of your USM masterclass constructed a tree-like reading room, an element midway between furniture and architecture inspired by nature. Why choose books as a way of rethinking modularity?

AW   I wanted to have my students explore a topic that seems so different from expected in the context of modularity. The book came to mind as a repository, a storage unit, or as a kind of shelving system for the philosophical, the emotional, the factual, the fictional, the poetic and the scientific. What each book has in common—what we might think of as the module—is the cover, the paper and the binding. The book allows authors with different minds, timeframes and geographical origins to be placed side by side, thus creating a library. The other day, we were talking about why so many architects feel the need to design a chair. The chair situates an architect in the context of culture and history. A chair is like the cover or pages of a book: it's a standard. The seat is 18 inches [46 centimetres] off the ground. It supports your body weight. You can lean your back on it. It has structure. If I examine a chair by Le Corbusier next to a chair by Frank Lloyd Wright, I'm not looking at the function or structure of these chairs: I'm looking at their different personalities. The requirements of the chair, like an algebraic formula, are the same for Wright and Le Corbusier.

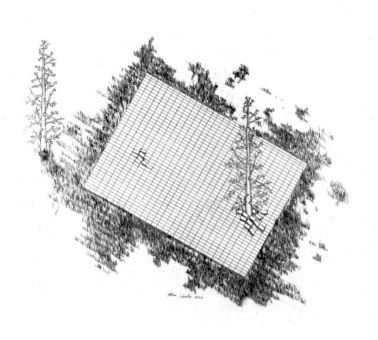

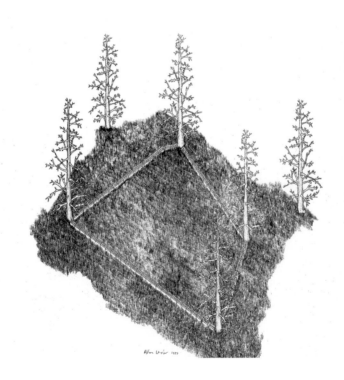

↑ Allan Wexler, 'Axonometrics
of the House', drawing, 1979

→ → Allan Wexler, 'Levittown
House Proposals', mid-1970s

Do you still work within that system, using standardized materials, or are you trying to expand or critique it in such a way as to challenge the system itself?

AW    If I have any doubts about using scale model props for my new photo-based pictures, I will choose my old standbys of 4 × 8 plywood panels, or 2 × 4s. However, I would interpret my use of tiled photos, which produce a superimposed grid over the complete image, as a form of modularity. Here the grid is used as a marking device, to help measure the complexities of a landscape's changing surface. The grid simplifies the complex, making order out of chaos. Whether I'm investigating ways to transform trees into lumber, elevate natural landscapes into the sky or mess with the daily rituals associated with eating, sleeping and bathing, I use the scientific method. I make one transformation at a time, document its results and move on to another transformation that results in another image, building, utensil, chair or sculpture. I work like a biologist who inserts one germ at a time into the same culture in a petri dish in order to understand one specific reaction. Here, methodology might be considered a modular means to carry out research. Let me see if I can stretch your definition of modularity and the use of standardized materials even further. I have discovered that my new works have universal stories, truths and archetypes embedded in them. I now intend to use ancient mythology and creation stories as inspiration. The myth is an armature that allows me to plug in my own contemporary and site-specific personality. The myth is the shelving system within which I can store my personal stories and particular personality.

In what way are you interested in 'beginnings' nowadays? How far does your new approach relate to modularity or your earlier work?

AW    With my new work I'm exploring man's first actions and interactions with the landscape. A shovel is forced into the ground. We lift earth skywards. We turn solid into void into solid. My photo-based images define these first acts, taking you on a journey through an invented history of architecture and civilization. They help you see the non-visible, to

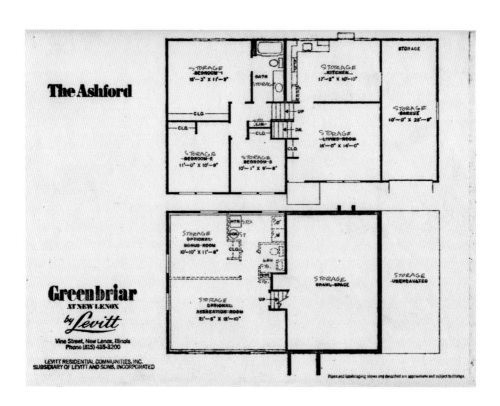

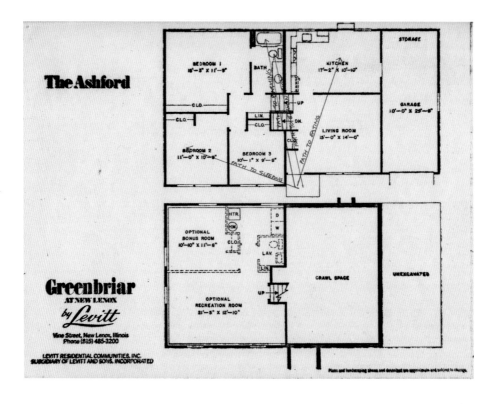

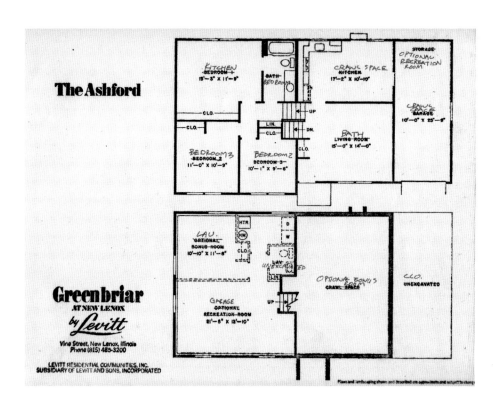

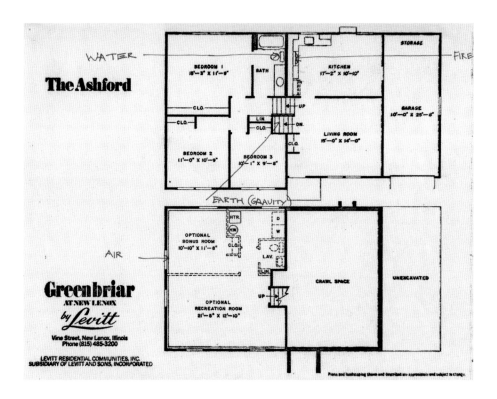

hover somewhere between the distant and
the intimate, to question the acts of drawing
and photography, and to see the ancient in the
contemporary. These new works consist of twelve
square photographs abutted and glued together
in a Cartesian grid to make one large image.
I allow some of the glue to seep out between each
photograph: this highlights the modular aspect of
the work and creates a grid in an attempt to make
order out of the complexity of civilization. The images
begin with landscapes sculpted from plaster and
white museum-board. The plaster, the chisel, the
scrapers and the files become my soil, shovel and
rake. The photo captures a memory.

11                                 Alongside the project you developed with your
masterclass, you also displayed historical,
contextual work at the 'rethink the modular'
exhibition. Please tell us about that. It obviously
focuses on the idea of the modular, but it is also
a critique of a certain modular housing system.

AW   It is a critique. I was very honoured to show
in the company of two my former teachers: Adolfo
Natalini from Superstudio and Michael Webb
of Archigram. My education at the School of
Architecture at the Rhode Island School of Design
was very much influenced by Superstudio and
Archigram. I somehow come out of that tradition of
experimenting with architecture and not necessarily
wanting to add more buildings to society, but
wanting to use my art to critique architecture.
Another project I produced took the floor plan of
a house from Levittown in the United States, which
was a very important landmark in the history of
housing development. William Levitt was a developer
of houses in the late 1940s, when soldiers coming
back from war had no place to live. He started
making these very simple, archetypal peaked-roof
houses in Levittown, Long Island. I have a plan of
a Levittown house that I photocopied many times
and, using a red marker, I transformed each of these
houses into a module. I rearranged rooms without
having to rearrange them physically. I would just
cross off the word 'bedroom', 'kitchen' or 'dining
room' and rearrange the rooms just by relabelling
them. I also tried to introduce elements of ancient

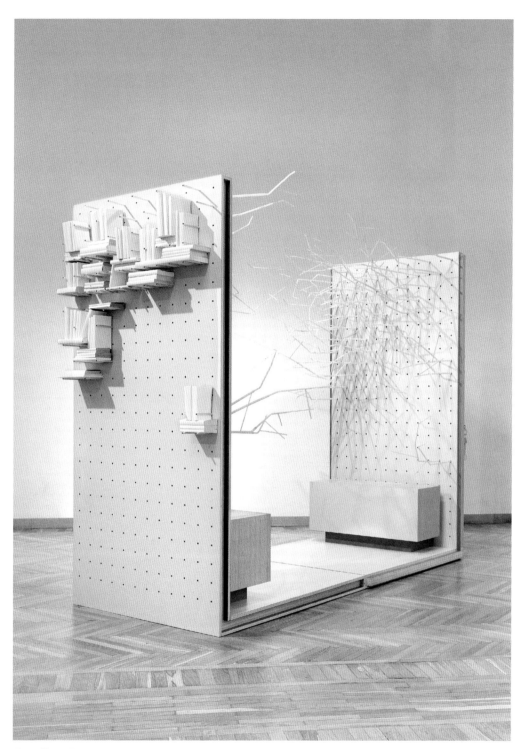

'Book/Store' by Allan Wexler's masterclass,
exhibition view in Milan, 2015

Allan Wexler, 'Proposal for Manhattan Skyline,
World Trade Center', 1973–76

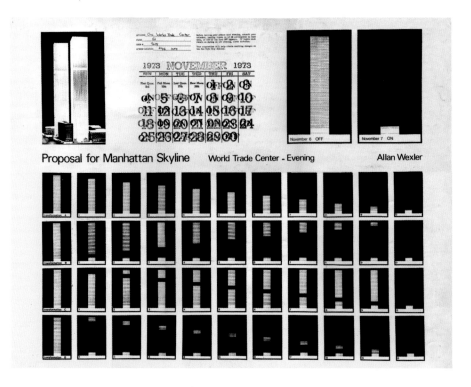

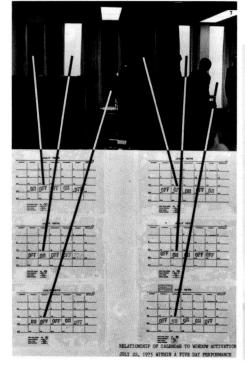

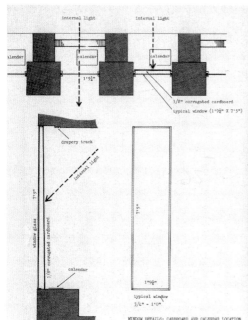

WINDOW DETAILS; CARDBOARD AND CALENDAR LOCATION

ritual by taking diagrams of initiation rites and ceremonies and superimposing them over the floor plan of a Levittown house. They are things that still interest me—the idea of imposing ritual ceremony over contemporary culture, because we have our own rituals in our domestic environments, when we drink coffee in the morning, wake up or read a book.

So this is a modern place, but it's also a sacred place? That's very far removed from notions of standardizing. It shows how flexible, how spiritual modularity can be.

AW  Well, that's how standardization, ritual and ceremony are: they're a type of modularity in a way. The Japanese tea ceremony is prescribed in great detail, and yet it's very spiritual. There are certain ways in which to hold and wipe the tea bowl or address your host or guest. Yet there is also a lot of metaphysical, spiritual and psychological content. All of the things that we think are the inverse of modularity are in fact a 'sideways vibration' occurring somewhere between modularity, science, mathematics and spirituality.

So we can describe modularity as a necessary condition for the sacred?

AW  Absolutely. I think so, yes.

Allan Wexler, one of the tutors of seven USM masterclasses, was interviewed during the 'rethink the modular' workshop at the Domaine de Boisbuchet, France, 2014 (I), and on the occasion of the 'rethink the modular' exhibition in Milan, 2015 (II).

# THE
# MODULAR

1

3

2

# CO-EXISTENCE

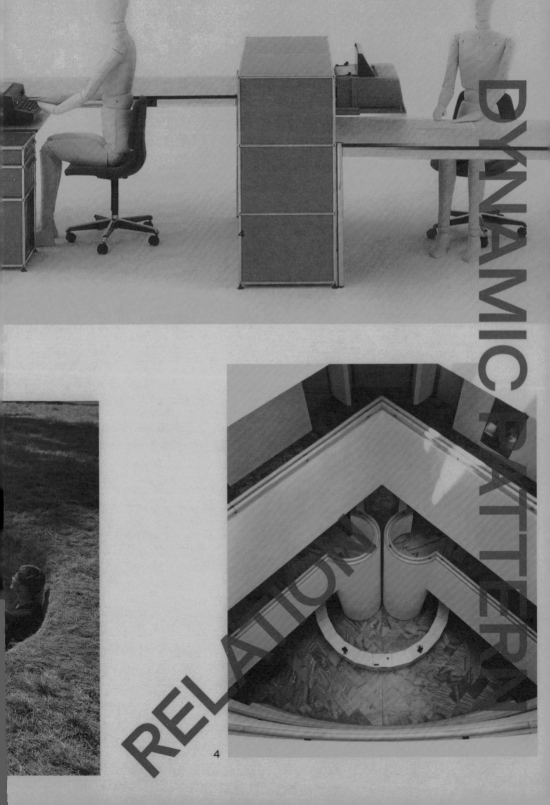

DYNAMIC PATTERN

RELATION

4

6

# CONSCIOUSNE

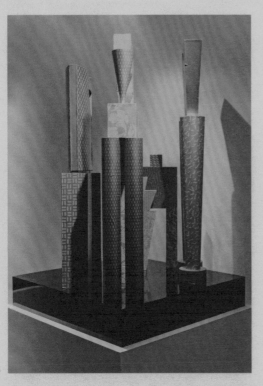

5

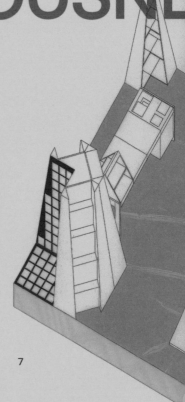

7

ESS

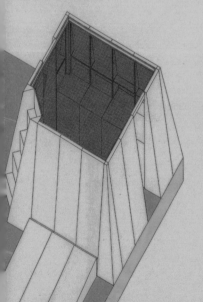

SURFACE

8

ATMOSPHERE

9

10

11

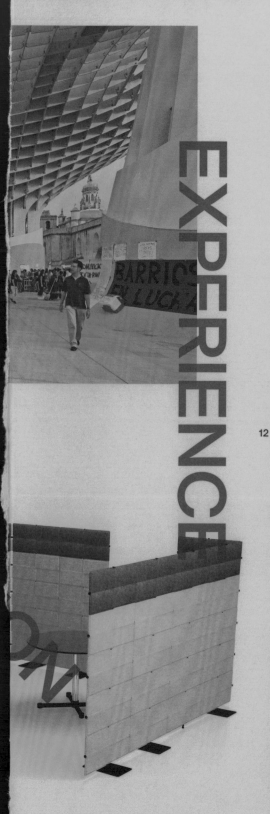

1 Superstudio, Istogramma, 'Lunch and Sleep', 1969
2 Go Hasegawa masterclass, 'Hole', 2014
3 USM Haller, Product catalogue for IT-integrated Workstations, 1994
4 USM Haller, Circular Counter for a bank building by Mario Botta, Lugano, 1995
5 Matteo Thun, 'The Heavy Dress–Fashion Tower', 1986
6 Cini Boeri, 'Serpentone' sofa, 1971
7 Gae Aulenti, 'Axonometric of Three Elements', 1972
8 Gio Ponti with Pier Luigi Nervi, Pirelli Highrise, drawing, 1958
9 USM Modular Furniture Haller in an open plan office, Cologne, 2001
10 J. Mayer H. Architects, 'Metropol Parasol', Seville, 2011
11 USM Privacy Panels, Prototype rendering, 2015
12 Dimitri Bähler masterclass, 'Networks in Motion', exhibition view Milan, 2015

EXPERIENCE

12

# The Modular

Squaring up to Superstudio: 126
Grids, Modularity and
Utopianism in Italian
Radical Design
Catharine Rossi

It's More Like a Service 154
Bless

From Functional Object to Icon: 168
The Changing Face of the USM
Haller System in Advertising
Martino Stierli

Dynamic Labyrinth (Seoul) 188
Rem Koolhaas,
Hans Ulrich Obrist

I Try To Be Architecture 208
Go Hasegawa

Wide Minds 220
Alva Noë

Calling Someone in China 236
Dimitri Bähler

Modularity and Adaptation 250
Thomas Dienes,
Jürgen Mayer H.

For a Tree, Modularity 270
is Not an Issue
Lorenzo Bini

When it comes to perceiving the world around us, modularity is not a technical approach but a prerequisite for action. Catharine Rossi discusses the architecture of Superstudio and other groups to show how the Italian Radical design movement of the 1960s and 1970s, and the utopian architectural design of the same period, simultaneously adopted a critical attitude towards modular structures and elevated them into icons. The reinvention of the modular as a visual language in architecture, advertising and design since the 1970s is tackled by Martino Stierli, who uses the example of USM Modular Furniture Haller and its representation in advertising.

We perceive modularity in our environment and even within ourselves. But how does digitalization effect our perception of interior and exterior spaces? Thomas Dienes and Jürgen Mayer H. discuss the extent to which it could lead to more flexibility in the uses of architecture and furniture. Rem Koolhaas and Hans Ulrich Obrist speak of the contemporary city as a dynamic labyrinth of material and media interfaces, while Alva Noë views perception not as something that is limited to our own heads, but as a network of interactions with our surroundings.

Interviews with Go Hasegawa, Dimitri Bähler, Bless and Lorenzo Bini, tutors of the USM masterclasses, explore our relationships with electronic media, designed space and the environment. As part of the 'rethink the modular' initiative, designers and architects from around the world were invited to think about these topics in a workshop at the Domaine de Boisbuchet, France, and to develop new projects for an exhibition in Milan.

# CATHARINE ROSSI

# SQUARING UP TO SUPERSTUDIO

# Squaring Up to Superstudio: Grids, Modularity and Utopianism in Italian Radical Design

## Catharine Rossi

Not many designers promote their furniture by photographing it in a field. Published in *Domus* magazine in 1972, one unusual campaign depicts cows, children and adults in the verdant Italian countryside, posing with a collection of wooden furniture—wardrobes, tables, stools, shelving units and a bed.[1] The objects' multiple functions are united by their pared-down formal and surface vocabulary. Every surface of these simple geometric volumes is covered with monochrome gridded plastic laminate, the number and distribution of the squares helping to define the outline of the furniture and lending it a standardized austerity that makes the pastoral setting even more surreal.

Designed in 1969 by Superstudio, the 'Misura' furniture that featured in the magazine was put into production by the Milanese producer Zanotta in 1970 as the 'Quaderna' series, with the plastic laminate specially produced by the Piedmont firm PRINT.[2] It forms one of the few furniture collections realized by Superstudio, the Florentine group who were one of the protagonists of Radical

1  *Domus*, no. 517 (December 1972), pp. 36–38.
2  See the Zanotta website: http://www. zanotta.it/#/en/products/Other_ Furniture/710_Quaderna.htm [last accessed 13 March 2015]. The plastic laminate had been designed for the exhibition *The Invention of the Neutral Surface*, conceived by PRINT (later known as Abet Laminati) in 1969 but never realized. See Peter Lang and William Menking, *Superstudio: Life Without Objects* (Milan: Skira; London: Thames & Hudson, 2003), p. 115.

design. Active in Italy from the mid-1960s to late 1970s, the Radicals sought to liberate architecture and design from their entrapment in a market-orientated, dead-end branch of modernism and transform them into utopian tools for Marxist-informed societal change. Much of this activity was carried out on paper and publicized in the architecture and design press, making the furniture's actual physical existence even more unusual.

Included in several international museum collections and still in production today, the furniture speaks of the ever-growing appetite for Radical design.[3] In recent years the avant-garde has been celebrated in several exhibitions and publications, and has inspired new products and new generations of socially and politically motivated designers.[4] Yet, despite the fact that it has received a great deal of public attention, key aspects of the movement remain insufficiently addressed. They include one of the defining features of the Misura furniture range: its modular grid-based design.[5] Misura was not the only instance when this design feature made an appearance. Occasionally on its own, but often combined with the grid, modularity was a persistent presence in Radical design. It appeared repeatedly in the projects, images and installations created by Superstudio and other individuals and groups associated with the avant-garde and the critical attitude it represented, from Archizoom Associati and Global Tools to Ettore Sottsass, Joe Colombo and Gae Aulenti. In 1960s and 1970s Italian design, if you wanted to be radical, you went modular.

This essay examines the modular in Radical design, with a particular focus on grid-based systems. It considers the existence of these intertwined tropes across multiple media, scales and functionalities, and reflects on the meanings of this multi-faceted mobilization in a context defined by the demise of modernism. As will become clear, the Radicals' use of a design system associated with such modernist ideals as standardization and universality was not about continuing the modernist movement's approach but, rather, reconceiving what the modular could offer: a combination of consistency and change that makes the concept of modularity still relevant for architects and designers today.

3   The furniture is included in various museum collections, including the Museum of Modern Art, New York, the Triennale Design Museum in Milan and the Museum for Applied Arts, Cologne.

4   The Radicals' recent appearances include the 14th Venice Architecture Biennale in 2014. See Alex Coles and Catharine Rossi (eds), *The Italian Avant-Garde: 1968–76* (Berlin: Sternberg Press, 2013).

5   One critic who has addressed this aspect of the furniture is the architectural historian Ross K. Elfline, whose research into Superstudio includes an interest in grids. See Elkfine, 'A Tentative Embrace: Superstudio's New Media Nomads', in *Regarding the Popular: Modernism, the Avant-Garde and High and Low Culture*, ed. Sascha Bru, Laurence van Nuijs et al. (Berlin: de Gruyter, 2012), pp. 458–70.

Misura was not the first project for which Superstudio had turned
to the modular language of the grid. Grids had been a hallmark
of both the two- and three-dimensional designs produced by
the group's six young architects, who first came together in 1966
at the architecture faculty of Florence University, a hotbed of
Radical design activity.[6] In fact, the furniture was the physical
manifestation of the group's 'Histograms'. Conceived in 1968,
this series of drawings depicted a system of gridded vertical bars.
These were to form the basis for design and architectural solutions
at any scale, from furnishings up to city level. The series expressed
a pared-down approach in which the architect had just to pick
the number of units needed to create the desired function. It could
not have been any more straightforward. As a young Rem
Koolhaas admiringly described in a letter to Superstudio member
Adolfo Nataliani, the Histograms were 'easy architecture'.[7]

The simplicity of the Histograms design tool was deliberate.
It expressed what the architects described as 'a precise wish to
reduce design operations to a strict minimum'.[8] Such minimization
would eventually lead to the eradication of their involvement—
which was why the series was also called 'The Architects' Tombs'.[9]
Their desire could appear at odds with conventional expectations
surrounding the architect's creative input, yet this suicidal impulse
was at the core of their thinking at the time. The Histograms
were monuments to a profession the group believed had outlived
its usefulness. This formed part of a broader discussion about
the 'death of architecture' in Italy; amid the failures of modernist
utopianism, buildings were seen as unable to solve society's
problems and adequately provide new ways of living.[10]

This concern underpinned Superstudio's work more generally.
As they explained in the *Domus* article that accompanied the
Misura photographs: 'It became clear to us that to continue
drawing furniture, objects and other similar household decorations
was not the solution to the problems of living in houses. Neither
was it the solution to the problems of life itself, and even less did
it serve to save one's soul.'[11] Both the Histograms and the Misura

6   Adolfo Natalini and Cristiano Toraldo
    di Francia set up Superstudio in 1966.
    Alessandro and Roberto Magris and
    Alessandro Poli joined in 1967, and Piero
    Frassinelli joined in 1968, completing
    the group.
7   Pier Vittorio Aureli, 'Manfredo Tafuri,
    Archizoom, Superstudio, and the Critique
    of Architectural Ideology,' in *Architecture*
    *and Capitalism: 1845 to the Present*,
    ed. Peggy Deamer (Abingdon and
    New York: Routledge, 2014), p. 142.
8   Lang and Menking, p. 115.
9   Ibid.
10  Andrea Branzi, *The Hot House: Italian New*
    *Wave Design*, trans. C. H. Evans (London:
    Thames & Hudson, 1984), pp. 53, 58.
11  *Domus*, p. 36.

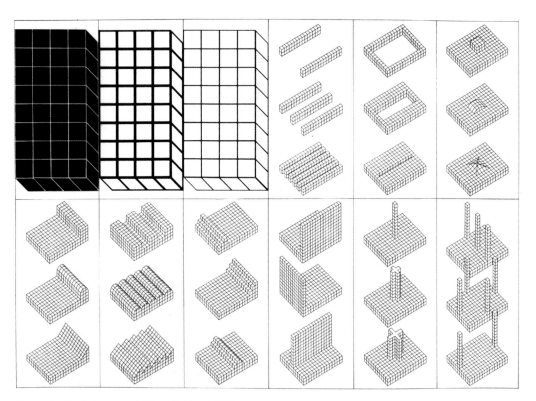

Superstudio, 'Istogrammi d'Architettura', 1971

series thus represent a transitional moment in Superstudio's practice. Amid a declining faith in real-world possibilities for architecture and design, the group were beginning to reduce not only the number of objects they designed, but also the role of objects in their design activity. They continued to produce drawings into the 1970s, but these were no longer precursors to manufactured objects or built architecture: the drawing became the end in itself. Amid this shift, the modular grid became even more prominent.

## THE CONTINUOUS MODULAR GRID

The use of grids to attack the modernist architectural avant-garde was most explicit in one of Superstudio's best-known works, 'The Continuous Monument'. Initially presented as a series of spectacular collages at *Trigon 69*, an international architecture exhibition held at Graz in 1969, the project was developed into a comic-style storyboard reproduced in *Architectural Design*, *Casabella* and *Domus* by 1971.[12] The name said it all. The Continuous Monument was a linear monolithic form that extended

12  See Marie Theres Stauffer, 'Utopian Reflections, Reflected Utopias', A A *Files*, no. 47 (2002), p. 25; Lang and Menking, p. 20.

Superstudio, 'Misura furniture' prototypes,
1969. Produced by Zanotta as the
'Quaderna' series, 1970.

through space, carving through natural and man-made landscapes from mountains to Manhattan, leaving the landscape on either side untouched. Its surface appearance varied: it was occasionally unadorned but mostly a monochrome grid; and it was either opaque, reflecting passing clouds in the sky above, or translucent, revealing glimpses of the terrain swallowed up by the infinitely repeating unit.

Just like the Histograms, the Continuous Monument proposed a universally applicable design solution. The architectural historian Marie Theres Stauffer describes its design methodology as based on 'a single unit that could be applied anywhere and that could be used to produce an infinitely repeatable, completely uniform architectural structure'.[13] Superstudio described their rationale in *Domus*, accompanying their explanation with illustrations of their research into the history of monuments:

> For those who, like ourselves, are convinced that architecture is one of the few ways to realize cosmic order on earth, to put things in order and above all to affirm humanity's capacity for acting according to reason, it is a 'moderate utopia' to imagine a near future in which all architecture will be created with a single act, from a single design capable of clarifying once and for all the motives which have induced man to build dolmens, menhirs, pyramids, and lastly to trace (ultima ratio) a white line in the desert.[14]

Superstudio thus presented the Continuous Monument as the culmination of an architectural evolution that had begun with Neolithic tombs, and also as the latest chapter in modernism's progressive utopianism. This is evident in the grid, famously identified by the art historian Rosalind Krauss as the 'emblematic' structure of the modernist avant-garde.[15] First appearing in French Cubism, the motif of the grid spread through Russian Constructivism and Dutch De Stijl in the early 20th century to become the ultimate modernist signifier. The apparent lack of historical or cultural references in its abstract, rational and universally recognized form was construed as signalling an original purity, a 'ground zero' for creative and societal renewal.[16] With their Continuous Monument, Superstudio simply extended the movement's rationalist logic to the whole world. Their grid-based module effaced existing architecture to allow all of mankind to enjoy the equal distribution of this rationally organized space.

13  Stauffer, p. 25.
14  Superstudio's 'The Continuous Monument: An Architectural Model for Total Urbanization' (1969). See Lang and Menking, p. 11.
15  Rosalind Krauss, *The Originality of the Avant-Garde and Other Modernist Myths* (Cambridge, Mass.: MIT Press, 1986), p. 9.
16  Ibid., p. 158.

The Continuous Monument echoes international architecture's megastructural tendencies of the late 1950s and 1960s, when the likes of the British group Archigram, the Japanese Metabolists and even fellow Radicals Gruppo 9999 conceived mobile architectural structures composed of infinitely rearrangeable and extendable standardized units.[17] By the early 1970s, however, as the British architectural critic Reyner Banham identified, megastructures had largely been abandoned in favour of 'more modest' solutions.[18] This chimed with some of the more negative readings of the Continuous Monument. Fellow critic Charles Jencks described the idea of taking modernist ideology to its 'logical conclusions' as 'absolute egalitarianism'; indeed, he employed Superstudio's own words to describe its ambitions for 'total urbanization' as 'Fascist'.[19] Yet, as Jencks's mobilization of the group's own description indicates, Superstudio recognized the authoritarian undertones of their grid-based utopianism. They knew the grid was not neutral but a highly charged modernist trope. Its use was subversive: in taking modernism's love of the grid to its extremes, they wanted to show up the movement's top-down, totalitarian ambitions and reveal the illogical, and undesirable, consequences of the world it had wanted to create. The subversive use of the modular grid was also apparent in the project that the Continuous Monument most directly inspired. Designed in 1969 by fellow Radicals Archizoom Associati, 'No-Stop City' was similarly conceived as an image-based architectural project that used, albeit in different ways, modularity and grids to describe a utopian vision.

## ARCHIZOOM AND ANTI-CAPITALIST ARCHITECTURE

Named after the British group Archigram, Archizoom followed a path that was closely connected with Superstudio's. Both groups were made up of young architects who had met at Florence University in the early 1960s.[20] They had emerged into the limelight at the same time through *Superarchitettura*, a self-curated exhibition of design objects that took place in Pistoia in 1966 and was repeated in a bigger context in Modena a year later.[21]

Grids had featured in Archizoom's work even before the group became officially established. In 1964 the architects had

---

17 Reyner Banham, *Megastructure: Urban Futures of the Recent Past* (London: Thames & Hudson, 1976), discussed in Ian Abley, 'Things Will Endure Less Than Us', in 'Manmade Modular Megastructures', special issue, *AD*, vol. 76, no. 1 (February 2006), p. 7; Gruppo 9999, *Ricordi di Architettura* (Florence: Capponi, 1972), p. 10.
18 Abley, p. 7.

19 Charles Jencks, *Modern Movements in Architecture* (Harmondsworth: Penguin, 1985), p. 56.
20 The founding members of Archizoom were Andrea Branzi, Gilberto Corretti, Paolo Deganello and Massimo Morozzi. They were joined in 1968 by Lucia and Dario Bartolini.
21 Branzi, pp. 52, 54.

→ Superstudio,
'Supersuperficie:
A Journey from A to B',
1971

↓ Superstudio,
'Monumento Continuo:
Alpine Lakes', 1969

→→ Archizoom
Associati (project
by Andrea Branzi),
'No-Stop City', model,
1969–2001

submitted 'La città estrusa' to a competition aimed at redeveloping the Piana di Firenze, a stretch of land separating Florence, Prato and Pistoia. As the title suggests, their design 'extruded' these cities together, turning the plain into what the architectural historian Pier Vittorio Aureli has described as 'one gigantic factory'.[22] This early project became the basis for their most celebrated work, 'No-Stop City'. Initially developed in response to Superstudio's 1969 Graz exhibit, it was first presented in *Casabella* a year later. Archizoom would return repeatedly to the project until 1972. It culminated in a series of photomontages, monochrome drawings and colour photographs of architectural models whose orderly distribution of a small family of identikit forms looked like a cross between a petri dish and a circuit board. Despite this microscopic appearance, No-Stop City shared the Continuous Monument's universalizing ambitions and its *reductio ad absurdium* logic. However, while both expressed a politically informed modernist critique, Archizoom was more violent in its anti-capitalist attack.

No-Stop City was an urban environment based on the architecture of the factory and the supermarket. These were presented as the two key architectural typologies of industrial capitalism: one for the production of commodities, the other for their consumption. As Archizoom member Andrea Branzi later described, both were 'potentially unlimited urban structures', since they overcame two constraints of conventional architecture: the need for natural light and ventilation.[23] Through the implementation of artificial lighting and ventilation, Archizoom could create a continuous environment in which the formal differences between architectural functions was erased and in which there was no escape from the all-dominant urban capitalist condition.[24] This was the capitalist logic taken to its nightmarish conclusion—a totally commodified condition that bears no small relation to contemporary society, in which nothing appears untouched by market forces.

Given their negative overtones, it could seem surprising that both Archizoom and Superstudio presented No-Stop City and the Continuous Monument as utopian projects. This was not contradictory. Rather, it reveals the specific brand of utopianism to which the Radicals adhered more generally, and which affirmed their difference to the earlier modernist avant-garde. Branzi explained that the Radicals did not propose the 'purely formal utopias' of Archigram and the Metabolists.[25] Instead, they offered what were variously called 'critical' or 'negative utopias'.[26] These

22 Pier Vittorio Aureli, 'More Money/Less Work: Archizoom', in Coles and Rossi, p. 150.
23 Branzi, p. 69.
24 Ibid., p. 72.
25 Ibid., p. 63.
26 Branzi, p. 63; Filberto Menna, 'A Design for New Behaviours', and Emilio Ambasz,

'Summary', in Emilio Ambasz (ed.), *Italy: A New Domestic Landscape: Achievements and Problems of Italian Design* (exh. cat., New York: Museum of Modern Art, 1972), pp. 412, 421.

utopias operated not by offering up a new world for contemplation, but by showing up what was wrong with the existing one. This approach often employed strategies of visual exaggeration, such as the excessive modularity of Archizoom and Superstudio's fictional worlds, to show up the real-world implications of capitalist and modernist ideologies. It is notable how amenable modularity and grids were to both 'formal' and 'critical' modes of utopianism, and to multiple ideological positions. They were a shifting but constant presence that in all cases spoke of the perceived agency and communicative potential of the modular motif.

## DOMESTIC MODULARITIES AND MODULAR DOMESTICITIES

Radical design's particular brand of utopianism contributed to the high level of international interest in the avant-garde in the 1970s. It even led to what was arguably one of the movement's biggest expressions of modularity: *Italy: The New Domestic Landscape: Achievements and Problems of Italian Design*, held at New York's Museum of Modern Art in 1972. Curated by Emilio Ambasz, an Argentinian architect who had joined the museum just a few years earlier, the exhibition is held up as a landmark in the history of both design and exhibition-making.

As Ambasz described in the catalogue, the aim of the exhibition was to 'recognize the cultural achievements of modern Italian design'.[27] These 'achievements' were two-fold: the 'remarkable' design of its products, which had ensured a high degree of commercial success, and the 'high level of critical consciousness' among Italy's architects that distinguished them from their international counterparts.[28] These dual character traits were broadly mirrored in the exhibition's two-part layout, divided into sections entitled 'Objects' and 'Environments'. Significantly, the display mechanisms of both were based on modularity. This made sense for two reasons: it could bring order to the diversity of contents, but it was also because *Italy: The New Domestic Landscape* was conceived as a touring show. Although the tour never happened, all of the display units had been designed for easy transportation and reassembly.[29]

'Objects' contained 180 highlights of domestic Italian furniture and product design from the previous decade. Alongside luxuries by celebrated architects such as Achille and Pier Giacomo Castiglioni and Gio Ponti, this section included early Radical

27 Ambasz, 'Summary', p. 419.
28 Ibid.

29 Pete Collard, 'Italy: The New Domestic Landscape', Disegno Daily, 28 November 2013. http://www.disegnodaily.com/article/italy-the-new-domestic-landscape [last accessed 14 March 2015].

designs by Archizoom and Superstudio, and products that displayed a broader interest in experimentation, particularly in terms of designing for the rise in informal and flexible lifestyles from the 1960s onwards. It included an emphasis on modularity, as in Joe Colombo's 'Tube Chair' (1969), made of 'nesting and combinable' plastic tubular elements, and Cini Boeri's 'Serpentone' (1968), a black polyurethane foam sofa semi-divided into slender vertical segments: you simply chose how many you wanted to fit in your home.[30] These objects were all displayed outside in the museum's sculpture garden, individually housed in cuboid display cases-cum-shipping containers made from timber planks.[31] The containers spot-lit and isolated the objects, which made them look like precious artefacts cut off from their social contexts, expressing the commodified status of design that the Radicals were trying to reject.[32]

Located in the museum's darkened basement, the 'Environments' section was equally domestically orientated. It consisted of eleven visions for the future of the home commissioned from 'established' architects, who included Gae Aulenti, Mario Bellini, Joe Colombo and Alberto Rosselli, as well as a number of Radicals, such as Gruppo Strum, Archizoom, Ettore Sottsass and Superstudio.[33] The brief stipulated some practical considerations: each architect was given a space measuring 5 metres (16½ feet) square within which to design, and each installation had to be suitable for transportation and reassembly, both from Italy to the US and on the proposed tour.[34]

Ambasz allowed more variation in the conceptual elements of the brief. While all the architects were required to address Italy's shortage of adequate housing, they were invited to respond to the brief differently according to their position on design.[35] Those who still believed in design 'as a positive activity' were invited to suggest how it could respond to the changing lifestyles patterns of the 1970s, including increasing informality, through the use of new materials and production techniques. Proponents of 'counterdesign' (another term for Radical design) were invited to see their installations as manifestos for their 'strategies for cultural change'.[36] Ultimately, environments in both camps expressed critical positions towards conventional design practice. Several

30  *Italy: The New Domestic Landscape*, pp. 116, 121.
31  Ambasz, 'Acknowledgements', *Italy: The New Domestic Landscape*, p. 14.
32  Rose DeNeve, 'Supershow in Retrospect: Review of *Italy: The New Domestic Landscape*', *Print*, November 1972, p. 67, cited in Felicity Scott, 'Italian Design & The New Political Landscape', *Analyzing Ambasz*, ed. Michael Sorkin (New York: Monacelli Press, 2004), p. 119.
33  Ambasz invited a total of twelve architects to design 'Environments'. Enzo Mari refused and instead submitted an essay to the catalogue. Two further proposals, by Gruppo 9999 and Gianantonio Mari, existed only on paper, the result of a competition for young architects to submit ideas.
34  *Italy: The New Domestic Landscape*., p. 142.
35  Ibid., pp. 143–46.
36  Ibid., pp. 137, 138.

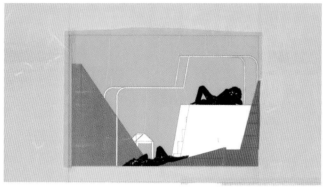

← Gae Aulenti, environment plan and section for *Italy: The New Domestic Landscape*, 1972

↓ Superstudio, Istogramma, 'Lunch and Sleep', 1969

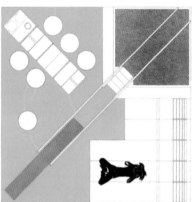

Gae Aulenti, environment
for *Italy: The New Domestic
Landscape*, 1972

architects also used modularity to do so, although largely in ways that often departed from the grid and its modernist associations.

Exponents of the first, 'pro-design' position included Aulenti, the only female architect commissioned to design an installation. Describing architecture as 'a positive thing', she argued that we should see the home not as composed of autonomous, isolated objects, but as an environmental element that revealed the connection between the private sphere of the home and the public space of the city. This desire to connect the self with society at large translated into a vision of the home as the city on a domestic scale. Her installation was composed of three different architectural components: one freestanding vertical shape, and two angled shapes (one wedge-like, the other with the profile of a stepped pyramid) that had to be used in combination with other elements to stand up. Made out of bright red fibreglass by Kartell and Zanotta, the large-scale architectural modules could be rearranged to become a range of different furnishings, from beds and cupboards to bookcases and seating.[37]

The flexibility and environmental emphasis that modular design enabled was also explored in Colombo's installation, the 'Total Furnishing Unit', which was realized by his studio following the young architect's death one year before the exhibition opened.[38] It still represented Colombo's vision, however, and it showed a significant shift in his design approach in the early 1970s. While modularity had been a key theme of earlier work, as in the 'Tube Chair', the architect was moving away from applying this thinking to the creation of individual objects and beginning to conceive coordinated design systems suitable for mass production.[39]

The Total Furnishing Unit consisted of four geometric volumes in white plastic with bright yellow doors and upholstery. Each 'unit' represented a different domestic component: kitchen, cupboard, bathroom and 'bed and privacy'. Diagrams in the catalogue indicated how they could be arranged in different configurations, according to the dimensions of the available space and the requirements of the inhabitants. This flexibility extended into the design of some of the units themselves, such that for 'bed and privacy', which served functions ranging from sleeping to socializing. This unit also featured a built-in television, anticipating how communication technologies would eventually penetrate into the very fabric of our domestic interiors.

As described in the exhibition catalogue, the Total Furnishing Unit's design was based on the principle of 'homogeneity'.[40] Its standardized elements were suitable for mass production, making a compact but flexible unit accessible to all—and demonstrating

37 Ibid., pp. 150–58.
38 Ibid., p. 14.

39 Ibid., p. 170.
40 Ibid., p. 172.

a combination of the standardized with the customizable that is being promised in today's 'third industrial revolution'. Its uniformity also discouraged excessive emphasis on any individual design elements, thus expressing Colombo's criticism of the commodified condition of the interior. Interviewed in *Casabella* in 1969, Colombo had attacked the idea that domestic interiors functioned merely to display 'taste, prestige, and so forth'. Instead, he argued for an 'anti-design' approach that opposed the 'glorification' of individual furnishings in favor of 'anonymous elements' that served real, primary needs.[41]

This use of modularity to critique commodity was most evident in Sottsass's installation. Despite the architect's Radical credentials, his work also appeared in Ambasz's first category—although it suggested his increasing uncertainty towards his profession's object orientation.[42] The installation consisted of identical vertically shaped grey plastic 'containers'. These self-described 'ordinary boxes' contained all necessary domestic elements, such as a stove, shower and storage cupboards. Inhabitants could choose to have as many or as few units as they needed, connect them with outlets to provide energy, water and air, and even move them around thanks to castor wheels on the bottom of each unit. Users could even choose to connect their elements with those belonging to friends and family, thereby creating community living environments as and when they wished.[43]

Like Colombo's, Sottsass's design relied on reconfigurable, standardized units. However, this was not because he envisaged mass production. In fact, the architect did not want to produce the units at all—and no one should want him to. Sottsass wanted to make furniture 'from which we feel so detached, so disinterested, and so uninvolved that it is of absolutely no importance to us ... so that after a time it fades away and disappears'.[44] This environment was another manifestation of the Radicals' critical utopianism: Sottsass designed exaggeratedly undesirable furniture in order to raise questions about consumer-based relationships with objects that had been designed to sate only superficial desires.

This anti-commodity stance was even more visible in the second of the two exhibition sections, 'Environments'— most notably in Superstudio's installation. 'Microevent/ Microenvironment' consisted of a dark room with a large plinth at its centre.[45] It supported a cube with polarized mirrored walls,

41  Joe Colombo in Carlo Guenzi, 'Cronache di Disegno Industriale', *Casabella*, February 1969, p. 28.
42  For more on Sottsass, see Philippe Thomé, *Sottsass* (London: Phaidon, 2014).
43  *Italy: The New Domestic Landscape*, p. 162.
44  Ibid.
45  *Italy: The New Domestic Landscape*, p. 242.

↑ Joe Colombo, 'Total
Furnishing Unit', environment
for *Italy: The New Domestic
Landscape*, 1972

↓ Cini Boeri, 'Serpentone'
sofa, 1971

→ Ettore Sottsass, environment
for *Italy: The New Domestic
Landscape*, 1972

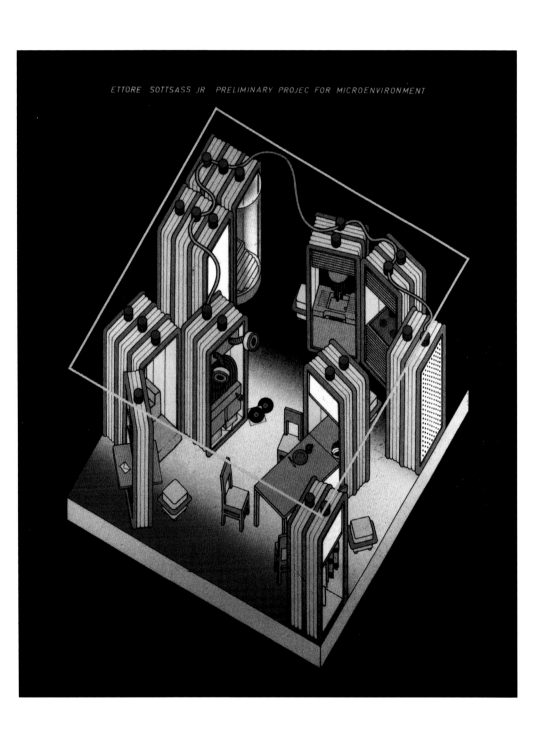

ETTORE SOTTSASS JR PRELIMINARY PROJEC FOR MICROENVIRONMENT

whose surfaces infinitely reflected the monochrome gridded design of the laminate floor inside the cube. In one corner of the room was a small box with wires sticking out, one of which led to a television showing a film on continuous repeat. Superstudio were one of several exhibitors to take up Ambasz's invitation to produce a film as part of their installation. Theirs combined footage set in the Italian countryside with more of the spectacular collages for which they had become known.[46] These collages depicted cut-out photographs of individuals and groups, from hippies to unhappy housewives. They were pasted over a perspectival grid with the same passing-clouds effect seen in images of the Continuous Monument, which here receded into a background of more cut-outs showing a variety of natural terrain that seemed to both define and be defined by the grid.

Superstudio described the installation as 'an alternative model for life on earth'.[47] This utopia expressed three key differences from earth as they knew it: no objects, no architecture and no work. It represented the elimination of any unsavoury qualities: there would be no status-symbol commodities, no built environments that perpetuated social inequalities, and no more alienating labour. Instead, all mankind would be free to enjoy a more meaningful existence devoted to what they termed 'conceptual activities (communications)' that would bring individuals into a closer, more meaningful connection with each other and the surrounding environment.

The grid was central to this vision. In the catalogue, the group described how it would gradually unfold to replace the world's architecture, becoming a pervasive phenomenon. The appeal to the grid's universalizing potential could seem surprising given Superstudio's earlier attempts to undermine this inherited modernist ambition. In reality, it reveals how much of the Radicals' ideas were actually defined in relation to modernism— even if it was done in order to visibly reject the earlier movement's ideas. It also suggests a continuing faith in the idea of the avant-garde, which itself was being questioned at the time, as is evident here in the group's ambition to restart society through the 'ground zero' grid.

This grid, however, also pointed to ways of thinking that went beyond the modernist avant-garde. Superstudio asserted that the 'Cartesian "squared" surface' should be understood 'not only in the physical sense, but as a visual-verbal metaphor for an ordered and rational distribution of sources'.[48] Specifically, the grid

46  For more on the films, see Peter Lang, 'Film and Counter Film: Moving Images from MoMA's *Italy: The New Domestic Landscape*', *Architecture Foundation*, 2013. http://www.architecturefoundation.org. uk/programme/2009/architecture-on-film/new-domestic-landscape [last accessed 16 March 2015].
47  *Italy: The New Domestic Landscape*, p. 242.
48  Ibid., p. 242.

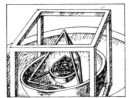

1. Keplero cercò di iscrivere dei solidi elementari nelle orbite dei pianeti.

**Kepler tried to inscribe elementary solids within the orbits of the planets.**

2. Vitruvio e Leonardo iscrissero l'uomo in un cerchio, gli indiani sistemarono il caos nel mandala.

**Vitruvius and Leonardo inscribed man within the circle, the Indians placed chaos within the mandala.**

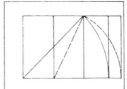

3. La sezione aurea, l'ordine, la simmetria erano insieme visione del mondo e mediazione per comunicare la natura delle cose.

**The golden section, order, symmetry, were at the same time a vision of the world, and a medium for communicating the nature of things.**

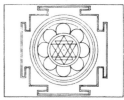

4. Il mandala come base per la meditazione è il tentativo di ordinare e dare un senso ad elementi divergenti.

**The mandala as a basis for meditation is a tentative try at ordering and giving a sense to diverging elements.**

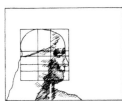

5. Il desiderio di rendere il mondo chiaro e distinto ha segnato tracciati regolatori sul viso umano e sul mondo...

**The desire to render the world clear and distinct has left regular paths upon the human face and on the world...**

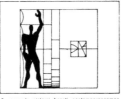

6. creando sistemi basati contemporaneamente sull'uomo e sulla geometria (come il Modulor).

**creating systems based at one and the same time upon man and upon geometry (such as the Modulor).**

7. L'uomo non è il centro delle cose, è solo uno dei vertici del poligono infinito che unisce cosmo, mondo, ragione.

**Man is not the centre of things, he is merely one of the vertices of the infinite polygon that unites the cosmos, the world, reason.**

8. L'astrologia collegava le manifestazioni umane agli astri; le scienze rivelano sempre nuove connessioni tra le parti e il tutto.

**Astrology connected human destinies and the stars; science is ever revealing further links between the parts and the whole.**

9. Le forme elementari sono la testimonianza di visioni del mondo. Dolmen, menhir, il sacro cerchio di Stonehenge, gli ziggurats...

**Elementary forms are witnesses to different visions of the world. Dolmen, menhirs, the sacred circle of Stonehenge, ziggurats...**

10. dei babilonesi e dei maya, le piramidi degli egiziani erano monumenti contro la morte, uno dei modi per sopravvivere, riconoscendosi.

**of Babylon and of the Mayas, the pyramids of Egypt were monuments against death, one way to survive, in recognizing oneself.**

11. Prendere coscienza del bisogno dei monumenti serve a colmare la frattura tra razionalità e inconscio: così si può osservare che...

**To realize the need for monuments is to fill in the fracture between rationality and the unconscious: thus one may observe that...**

12. la Kaaba e il Vertical Assembly Building sono due uguali cubiche pietre nere, egualmente monumentali.

**the Kaaba and the Vertical Assembly Building are two identical black stones, both equally monumental.**

13. Quando poi i segni umani non sono solidi elementari, sono lunghe linee continue, teorie d'elementi, espressioni di una...

**Then, when human signs are not elementary solids, they are long continuous lines, a theory of elements, the expression of...**

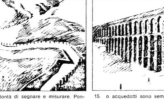

14. stessa volontà di segnare e misurare. Ponti, muraglie cinesi,...

**the same will to sign and measure. Bridges, Chinese walls,...**

15. o acquedotti sono sempre monumenti continui ugualmente allungati sulla terra per comprenderla.

**or acqueducts are still continuous monuments, also lying full length to embrace the earth.**

16. Così fino alle autostrade, alle dighe e ai grandi manufatti della tecnica in scala con le nuove dimensioni.

**And so on up to the motorways, great dams and huge products of technology on a scale with the new dimensions.**

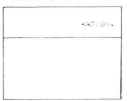

17. Dalla Genesi: «In principio Iddio creò il cielo e la terra, la terra era una cosa senza forma e vuota» - e poi dall'Apocalisse:

**From Genesis: «In the beginning, God created the heavens and the earth, and the earth was without form and void» - and then from the Apocalypse:**

18. «La città era un quadrato, e la sua lunghezza era uguale alla sua larghezza». Tutta la storia sta tra il caos e l'architettura.

**«And the city lieth foursquare, and the length is as large as the breadth»; and all history lies between chaos and architecture.**

19. La nostra storia è appunto una parabola di formalizzazione; così è una storia di deserti naturali ed artificiali...

**Our story is just a parable of formalization, so it is a story of deserts, both natural and artificial,...**

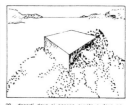

20. deserti dove si posano nuvole o dove nascono nuvole che poi generano apparizioni geometriche lungamente attese.

**deserts where clouds may come to earth or where clouds are born, then to generate geometrical, long-awaited apparitions.**

Superstudio, storyboard for a film about the 'Continuous Monument', *Casabella*, no. 358, 1971

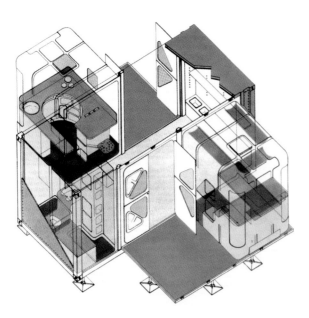

Richard Sapper and Marco Zanuso, 'Mobile Housing Unit', environment for *Italy: The New Domestic Landscape*, 1972

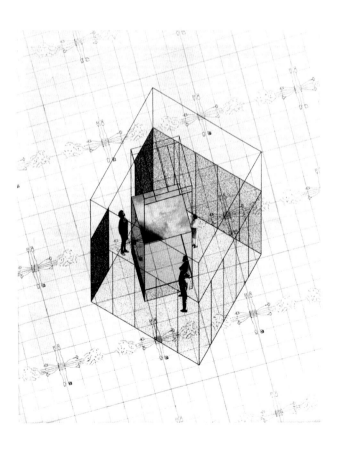

Superstudio, 'MicroEvent/
Microenvironment', environment
for *Italy: The New Domestic
Landscape*, 1972

signified 'a network of energy and information' evenly and equally distributed to all. Just as in the Continuous Monument, the grid would connect all the earth's inhabitants and erase all inequalities between them—only this particular grid would do so through the unifying potential of technology rather than the modernist monolith. The architecture-less, nomadic inhabitants of Superstudio's grid did not need buildings to consider themselves at home: they could plug in at any time and at any point, instantaneously connecting them to all the other dwellers of this utopian vision.

Through this technologically driven scheme of global integration, Superstudio had created what the media theorist Marshall McLuhan—a key inspiration for the Radicals—termed the 'global village'.[49] Writing in *Understanding Media* (1964), McLuhan described how, 'after more than a century of electric technology, we have extended our central nervous system itself in a global embrace, abolishing both space and time as far as our planet is concerned'.[50] Superstudio had realized McLuhan's vision for a technologically permeated future in which the self had expanded into a global society, which had in turn contracted to the level of the individual self.

Superstudio offered the fullest expression of the modular grid as a network in the New York exhibition. It was also present in other installations—in Colombo's integrated television, Sottsass's plug-in units and Aulenti's desire for a home that was connected to the wider environment. These Italian examples were in turn part of an increasing international interest in networks that had arisen in the 1960s, and a belief that the significance of traditional architectural structures and environments would be replaced by the electronic, immaterial structures of communication technologies.[51] These visionary voices predicted a world in which differences between time and place would be erased—creating a condition of elasticity that we can recognize in our own digital age.

Modules, grids and now networks: the presence of these three tropes is not confined to the examples given here. In addition to the extensive experimentation carried out by Archizoom and Superstudio, they are evident elsewhere in the Radicals' output, from Marco Zanuso and Richard Sapper's transportable units for the 'Environments' section of *Italy: The New Domestic Landscape*, to the grid-based imagery created by the likes of Gruppo 9999 and Global Tools. Modularity, be it expressed through grids or used to express networks, could be seen as a defining trait of

49  Marshall McLuhan and Quentin Fiore, *The Medium is the Massage: An Inventory of Effects* (New York: Bantam Books, 1967), p. 63.

50  Marshall McLuhan, *Understanding Media: The Extensions of Man* (London: Routledge, 1964), p. 19.

51  Mark Wigley, 'Network Fever', *Grey Room*, no. 4 (Summer 2001), pp. 82–122.

Radical design as a whole, from its origins in the mid-1960s to the movement's demise in the late 1970s.

Modularity offered Italy's Radicals a means of thinking through and communicating their ideas. Its appearance changed in line with the movement's changing ideas, at times indicating a continuing, if contradictory, dialogue with modernism, and at others signalling a new conversation with communication technologies that is becoming only more relevant today. The constantly connective, coordinated qualities of modularity enabled these changing conversations—resulting in a flexible consistency that meant modularity could be applied on virtually any scale or to any design scenario, and an efficiency that ensured nothing was wasted in the message being communicated. These two qualities in themselves would be enough to justify the ongoing relevance of modularity today, particularly given the need to reduce waste in a context of increasingly scarce resources. What is most apparent in the Radicals' turn to modularity is its mobilization to communicate a desire for change; and change in itself is inherent in modularity, given the ever-evolving nature of the units on which it is based, from the metres and litres of an analogue world to the pixels and megabytes of today's digital culture. It is ultimately this forward-looking and adaptable characteristic that has made the universal concept of the modular so valuable for designers thinking and rethinking the meaning and potential of their practice in the past, present and future.

BLESS

IT'S MORE
LIKE A
SERVICE

## It's More Like a Service

## Interview with Bless and
## Marlene Oeken

I

INTERVIEWER  One of the recurring motifs in your work is the hammock, which you've created in various forms and materials. How do you adapt this to different cultures? Do you see it as a modular element in your designs?

BLESS  In general, the hammock stands for relaxation and free time devoted to musing. Most people connect it with holiday experiences of sun and siestas in southern countries. It would have been problematic to introduce this holiday souvenir item into a living environment at home because of its ethnic connotations. It would have resembled something foreign that had been imported but not really been adapted for our culture. We preserved only the functional element, therefore, modifying the hammock's appearance in terms of its materials and shape so that it would correspond better with an urban, Northern European culture. With this aim in mind, we produced a series of hammocks that introduced the 'holiday' element into the environment of city living—think of the 'Sofa Hammock', which looks like some sort of suspended sofa with geometrically shaped cushions. We first presented the hammocks in connection with our Bless N°29 Wallscape project and the N°28 collection, both of which are integrated into a living environment.

In a sense, you could speak of all the Bless editions in modular terms, if you understand modularity as a way of connecting—not only things, but also cultures or different ways of living.

↙ Bless shop, Berlin, 2012

↓ Bless, 'N° 28: Fur Hammock', installation view, 2006

So when you set up your work for an exhibition, you avoid showing just the hammock to avoid giving the impression that you're presenting it as a product. What do you show alongside it?

B    Actually, the real explanation lies in the way we number our collections, starting with Bless N°00. This is our rhythm, and within this rhythm we present whatever we've worked on during the last six months. We produce three numbers a year because most of the time there is just one important exhibition or special project we're working on, apart from two clothing collections per year. You can see each Bless number as a sort of bracket around a specific number of products that reflect our personal status quo at that very moment.

You mentioned a 'bracket' around a number of designs. Could you also see your project numbers working together as a modular system? Do you see some kind of connection between the numbers? Do they reuse and re-present elements from past collections?

B    Whatever product we create, be it a pair of
trousers or a chair, we love the idea that it ages with
us. After fifteen years of designing, instead of doing
something totally new we tend to pick aspects of
our old collections and redo them according to our
current tastes. That means we modify certain details,
but the design itself remains the same. Somebody
told us that his most beloved product, a cashmere
sweater, had holes. So we applied pearls to the
elbows. This season, we remade that pullover but
we applied different pearls, and the texture was
completely different. We often look back, reviewing
and refining what made sense at the time, and
seeing what we still like, establishing some classics
by and for ourselves. Following this approach, each
collection is composed of familiar as well as entirely
new modules.

Looking at Bless N°51, how do the different pieces in
the collection relate to each other? Are you interested
in some kind of cultural system, which you create
through your work?

B    Design in general has the potential to modify
cultural behaviour and ways of thinking, and can
exert a kind of social influence. It can solve problems
where the political system acts too slowly or is too
much driven by the economy. From our perspective,
we don't aim to create a cultural system but try
to establish a very personal microcosmos. To build
a made-to-measure profession seems to be the
healthiest option for us, and we would like to
encourage others to do the same.
    In each of our collections you will find clothing
pieces as well as design pieces. Together they define
our current worldview, like a screenshot. The N°51
collection contains new design pieces called 'Silent
Servants'—a title that would serve equally to describe
how we see ourselves and our profession. The 'Silent
Servants' are composed of different round brass
profiles that together form a modular system. They
feature different mechanisms to hold soft or hard
materials. They work like a kind of extended valet
stand, which you can use as a wardrobe or as a
display. These elements are useful for presenting
a collection quite naturally.

How would you describe your relationship with your customers and your audience? How do you establish a connection with your clients?

B    We discovered that we do presentations mainly for our clients. It's not our strongest point, being social, but it's good to do it twice a year at least. That's when we do our presentations and shows. A certain number of people follow our idea of repeating what we've already done ten years ago, because they like the fact that they don't have to try on a pair of trousers—they can just buy them blind, knowing it's their size, their style and they like the fabric. The clothing line mainly consists of pieces we developed a long time ago. It's interesting because we found a group of people who feel the same as us. We can't say we don't care about our clothes. On the other hand, we hate the whole process of shopping, trying on, etc. Instead we like to establish the kind of wardrobe you don't have to think about but can rely on in terms of style and quality. It has the same trousers that you already know will fit you. It's more like a service. That makes it easy for a lot of people who are interested in clothing and who like this reliable, repetitive element but are not necessarily into fashion to say: 'Please do this pullover again.' Actually, that's how we started. We teamed up, defined a common thread and offered the results to a certain kind of audience. That's what got the ball rolling. It is our way of communicating: the products we make, the service.

As far as your clothes are concerned, do you stick to certain patterns that you like, or are they a long-term exploration of form?

B    There's not so much thought behind it. It's simple: you have a pattern. When the next season arrives, you don't have to do something new because the pattern is still valid. Sometimes we modify the patterns and fine-tune them endlessly over the years. You really would not notice that some pieces have changed, but they do change every season. It's very hard to point to exactly what is important for our design or our work, because everything feels totally bound up with our lives. You could say that our overall aim is to become more efficient and more

Presentation by the Bless
masterclass at the Domaine
de Boisbuchet, France, 2014

→→ Bless, 'Nº 40: Workout
Computer', 2010–15, punchbag
keyboard, exhibition view, Milan,
2015

→→→ Bless masterclass,
'Exoteric Souvenirs', 2015

precise in defining our thoughts, statements and
tools, and in the meantime the results take the form
of lifestyle products.

You place great store by your collections as small,
self-contained systems that are not isolated products
so much as holistic snapshots of your design
philosophy. In what way do your Bless Homes in
Berlin and Paris—your down-to-earth showrooms
where Bless products are mixed with other everyday
items—represent your position?

B    There is always a strange gap between the way
you perceive products when you first encounter them
displayed in an artificial shop setting and the context
those products will live in later on once purchased.
The Bless Homes function as archive and storage
rooms—spaces to display typical interior products,
kitchens where you can cook things we like to taste
and share with others—but at the same time they're
meeting rooms for people who want to see objects
in real life or talk to us about their ideas and visions.
Sometimes we use the Bless Home as an addition to
our studios and private homes, offering it as a guest
room or apartment for friends and clients. They can
then take their time to try on things or spend one
night in our N°33 'workbed' wrapped in Bless sheets.
The Bless Homes should ideally facilitate encounters
between people and products.
     Over time we've learned that everything is
connected and equally relevant: the comfortable
atmosphere, true privacy shared between those
involved, good food and drinks. It's not about clothes
and design: it's more about sharing a moment in
the here and now, and offering what we consider the
most precious experiences when we travel: being
invited into people's homes.

II          The designers at Bless don't like to be in front of
            the cameras too much, but when you visit the
            exhibition they are everywhere. There's one group
            doing performances, and there's the Bless workout
            computer. The group is very present … so Bless
            did it again!

MARLENE OEKEN    Well, invisibility doesn't mean
that what we do doesn't have an effect. It's just not

about putting something straight on a pedestal. What we produced with the USM masterclass at the Domaine de Boisbuchet were actually instruments or wearable musical accessories that would naturally generate sound and rhythm. For example, I wore bracelets on both arms and little pieces of plastic sewn onto the seams of my trousers. Whenever I walked with my arms relaxed, they made a noise when they touched my legs. This automatically drew attention to my body, to the rhythm of my movements. Other instruments included a necklace that bounced on a stiffened t-shirt front when the wearer moved her torso back and forth; a mobile phone app encouraging the user to flip the device over; and a pair of gloves containing heavy metal balls and bracelets that generated sounds when you moved your wrist.

It seems that the project your group showed at the exhibition in Milan has undergone quite significant changes compared to its approach at the masterclass at the Domaine de Boisbuchet.

MO   We decided that what worked extremely well in Boisbuchet, an isolated place in the countryside, needed to be adapted for a new, more urban environment such as the Milan Furniture Fair. We therefore developed new tools for exhibition visitors, enabling them to share in our experience instead of us being the only performers. It turned out that 'rethink the modular' was just the starting point for us, and in Milan we have noticed a strong group dynamic encouraging this process of collaborative working. Bless no longer feel like teachers, but have become collaborators alongside the other participants. We have decided to work together as a group named 'Exoterika' beyond this project.

The group decided to focus on drinking glasses as appropriate, simple tools that every visitor could use at the various events that took place during the 'rethink the modular' exhibition in Milan. Five different glasses were created. First of all there was the 'Stoner', which incorporated a piece of rock as its foot. The second, 'You Can Say it Again', included a microphone that recorded snippets of conversation and sometimes broadcast them publicly into the courtyard of the exhibition space. 'Chaincheers' was a glass whose its stem was replaced by a chain. The fourth, named 'The Opening Hiker', was a long wooden stick supporting a glass at its tip, which allowed the drinker to wander around. Lastly, the 'Boirebuchet' was a glass sunk into a huge piece of heavy wood that amplified the gesture of drinking, making it necessary to use both hands.

Are these pieces about obstruction?

MO    No, the opposite: they help you to communicate with other people. If you want to have a drink using 'The Opening Hiker', the glass with the long stem, you really have to ask for space if you're in a crowded area. Likewise, when you're drinking with both hands and you want to smoke a cigarette or eat something, you have to ask somebody else to hold the glass for a second. In the end the glasses forced their users to modify pre-learned and automatic patterns of behaviour, and that's what we're interested in.

The design duo Bless were interviewed as tutors of one of the seven USM masterclasses held during the 'rethink the modular' workshop at the Domaine de Boisbuchet, France, in 2014 (I). Marlene Oeken, was a participant in the masterclass and was interviewed as a spokesperson for the team on the occasion of the 'rethink the modular' exhibition in Milan, 2015 (II).

FROM
FUNCTIONAL
OBJECT
TO ICON

# From Functional Object to Icon: The Changing Face of the USM Haller System in Advertising

## Martino Stierli

Fritz Haller's furniture system for USM is one of the great icons
of 20th-century design history. Needless to say, its functionality,
flexibility and potentially endless expandability, as well as the
rhetoric surrounding this legend of design, have helped it assume
this privileged position. Against such a functional argument,
I would like to contend that USM is also a particularly successful
manifestation of a certain political, social, cultural and economic
situation, and that it was only through this congruence that
Haller's ingenious invention could become what it is today.
Moreover, as I intend to demonstrate, the public perception of the
USM Haller system underwent a number of significant shifts and
adjustments, which were triggered not least by the way USM Haller
has been presented in the company's advertising campaigns over
time. By looking at these advertisements, it is possible to trace
the changing meaning of a design object over the course of half
a century, from a tool with which to organize corporate office
space to a fetishized object.

Fritz Haller first conceived his furniture system for the firm of
U. Schärer Söhne (later USM U. Schärer Söhne AG) in Münsingen,
Switzerland, in the early 1960s, as he was working on a design for
the company's new operational headquarters. He envisaged a
modular system that would be applied not only to the architecture,
but also to the building's furnishings—a total design, but without

any conspicuous 'design' features, so to speak. The underlying construction system, out of which the USM Haller system eventually evolved, was intended to be non-site specific and applicable anywhere in the world. In fact, it was a way of organizing and defining space by means of a radically limited number of prefabricated elements. One could see Haller's invention (the individual steps of which have been meticulously analysed and described elsewhere[1]) as a manifestation of Heidegger's notion of *Gestell*, implying an underlying technological apparatus in the sense of an endlessly expanding grid into which physical objects are placed.

Thinking of Haller's system in these terms reveals its two-fold universalism. On the one hand, it is much more than just a furniture system: it is a fundamental technological device to define and organize space, and, as a result, a conceptual tool to render such abstract notions of space concrete. On the other hand, it is a system that works within any conception of Euclidian space, irrespective of historical or cultural conditions. The fact that USM's invention dates to the early 1960s and thus to an age of strong universal aspirations (in the Western world in particular) hardly seems coincidental. Nor is it surprising that USM—most probably precisely because of this coincidence—rapidly established itself as the gold standard of corporate office aesthetics in the years of the Pax Americana with its universalist claims. It could be argued that USM Haller is the equivalent of Adrian Frutiger's Univers typeface of 1954, which also became a hallmark of post-war corporate culture. The same design ethos manifested itself in utopian architectural projects of the period as well: Superstudio's Continuous Monument project (1969), for instance, which is based on the relentless repetition of a cubic white module, superimposes itself on the natural landscape and thus underscores an aspiration to universally organize and define space irrespective of existing cultural or historical conditions.

USM Haller would thus appear to be the epitome of the universal spatial ambition of the 'organizational complex' displayed by capitalist bureaucracies of the post-war period.[2] If this were an accurate characterization of Haller's system, however, we would be unable to explain its continuing popularity right up to the present day. Indeed, the system—or, more precisely, its aesthetics—have proven remarkably adaptable throughout the decades, and it has succeeded in reinventing itself as a design solution that is both timeless and contemporary. USM Haller does not confine itself to

1   See Arthur Rüegg, '"Das definierte Nichts": Auf dem Weg zum perfekten Möbelsystem', in Laurent Stalder and Georg Vrachliotis (eds), *Fritz Haller: Architekt und Forscher* (Zurich: gta Verlag, 2015).

2   See Reinhold Martin, *The Organizational Complex: Architecture, Media, and Corporate Space* (Cambridge, Mass.: MIT Press, 2003).

USM Haller, 'Full Cockpit', USM Headquarters
in Münsingen, Switzerland, 1969

1960s retro nostalgia, in which respect it differs markedly from
other design icons of the period.

Nowhere, perhaps, is this remarkable contemporaneity
of USM Haller more evident than in the way the company's
advertising campaigns have presented it over the past fifty years.
In the following essay, I will set out to visually analyse a selection
of these advertisements in order to determine how USM Haller
has continuously altered the image of its product according to ever-
changing notions of what a contemporary working and/or living
space should be. In so doing, the company has also had a decisive
impact on how we, its customers, have imagined such spaces
over time. Through this continuous visual reinvention, USM has
added layers of meaning to the furniture system. Given that the
backdrop against which it has been presented is predominantly
(although not exclusively) the modern office, this inquiry also lends
itself to the question of how the workspace was conceived and

represented at the dawn of the information age. As labour has shifted from manual to intellectual, it has become increasingly invisible, and the creation of economic value has been sublimated into an abstract entity beyond the realm of conventional representation. As a consequence, many of the images advertising the USM company have the air of a crime scene—deserted, but full of traces of recent human presence and activity, as if to point to the underlying dilemma of representation. Moreover, the pictures also tell the story of early communication systems—another instance of the dematerializing and ephemeralizing of our everyday environment and its dissolution into a network of invisible constellations.

The furnishing of the company's office building in 1969 gave USM an early opportunity to demonstrate the ways in which the company foresaw the organization of contemporary corporate office space. The architectural stage set shows nondescript, generic interiors (see image 7, p. 286). Natural light is provided by the large floor-to-ceiling windows of a curtain-wall façade, whose blinds ensure its uniformity. We find ourselves in the transparent corporate architecture that, by the late 1960s, had become the new vernacular of the period—a lingua franca whose relentless repetition and seemingly all-encompassing dominance was humorously addressed in Jacques Tati's *Playtime* (1967). Indeed, the French director's masterpiece appears like a dystopian mirror image of the USM open plan office. If Tati imagined a corporate world in which everything and everyone is reduced to shades of grey, the colourful surfaces of USM Haller provide an air of optimism and cheerfulness. Individual workspaces are conceived as populated islands in a seemingly endless expanse of continuous space, and the furniture of the USM Haller system functions as a spatial divider and definer very much in the way a wall would in a more traditional architectural set-up. This is the quintessential open-floor office environment in which it is the furniture that lends spatial structure and invokes a sense of ready changeability. As if to counter the potentially discomforting psychological effects of such an open, uniform working environment, the components of the USM Haller system are arranged to form pockets of cosy embrace. This is most evident in what appears to be the workplace of an executive: while the green USM Haller sideboard forms a wall-like barrier against the backdrop, the smaller, orange pieces are placed obliquely and in seemingly impromptu fashion, subverting the relentless orthogonality of the space, as if to suggest that this furniture too can produce a homely atmosphere. The system's flexibility is communicated in two ways: the images emphasize both the mobility of individual elements (which are on wheels) and the multi-functional uses to which they might lend themselves. An open book, a pair of glasses and an extinguished pipe in an ashtray

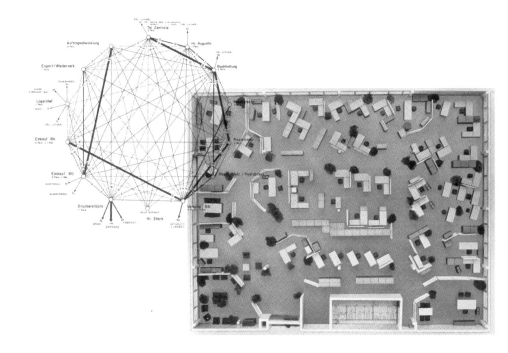

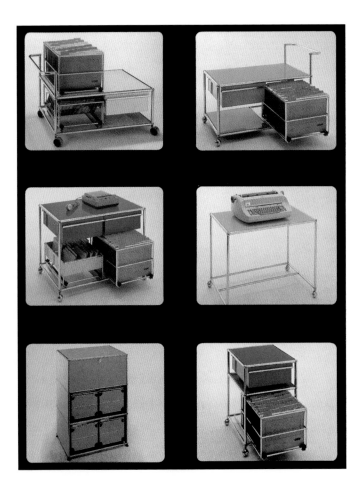

↑ USM Haller, 'Teamland',
open-plan office concept,
Zurich, 1973

← USM Haller, file storage
from the 1970 product
catalogue

point to recent human presence, while also reminding the viewer—at least as far as the pipe is concerned—of changes in rules governing acceptable workplace behaviour. The same is true for the glass of whisky on top of the green cabinet at the back, which apparently serves not only as storage for files, but also as a bar. It is as if we were looking at the suddenly deserted set of an episode of *Mad Men*.

As we move to USM Haller's self-representation in advertising of the 1970s, two aspects are conspicuous: first, the 'Teamland' documentation—an open-plan concept for offices developed by and for the Swiss company Rüegg-Nägeli + Cie AG, Zurich—illustrates that the furniture system has been used to organize the office in such a way as to maximize communication between different departments while at the same time minimizing the total area used for such an undertaking. This two-fold result is visualized through the pairing of an abstract geometrical chart illustrating the flow of communication and information with the model of an office space in which the furniture is a strategic device mapping this abstract diagram of relationships in spatial terms. Very much in line with contemporary network theories, the office space is understood as a network of communications and the flow of information.[3] Second, the photographs that illustrate this conception (see image 6, p. 286) include actual people working at their desks and at the filing cabinets, in stark contrast with the 'crime site' aesthetic of the previous decade. Thus, while the new devices of information technology, cybernetics and network theory have been applied to create an increasingly controlled work environment, the presence of office clerks in the photographs suggests that the design of the workspace is increasingly perfected to fit the needs of those working there. Technological control and a drive for efficiency are masqueraded as a humanizing of the workspace. It is the physical elements of the USM Haller system that make this ambiguous situation appear natural.

A second group of images from this period comes from a photo shoot undertaken in 1976. For the first time we find the USM Haller system in a home environment. The back of the set is dedicated to a home office, but the cabinets in the centre of the photo serve as spatial dividers, separating off the living-room atmosphere in the foreground, in which the coffee table is another example of the system's adaptability. Since the latter had made a triumphal entry into corporate office spaces around the world, the company's obvious aim was now to target new potential users and markets for its product. Rather than actual propositions for

3    See in this regard Mark Wigley, 'Network Fever', *Grey Room*, no. 4 (Summer 2001), pp. 81–122; Andreas Rumpfhuber, 'Space of Information Flow – The Schnelle Brothers' Office Landscape Buch und Ton' in Ákos Moravánszky and Albert Kirchengast (eds), *Experiments: Architecture Between Sciences and the Arts* (Berlin: Jovis, 2011), pp. 201–25.

↑↑ USM Haller, living room with home office, 1976

↑ USM Haller, doctor's surgery, 1976

↑↑ USM Haller, open-plan office, 1976

↑ USM Haller, director's office, 1976

a specific interior environment, another series of pictures from the same year and source look like conceptual blueprints for how the modularity of the USM Haller system could be applied to every aspect of an environment, from individual objects to the structure of walls and ceilings. More radically than before, these photographs suggest that the furniture system is capable of producing a completely autonomous world unto its own. The complete auto-referentiality of this proposition is reflected by the absence of any apertures that open onto an outside world. We are reminded of utopian/dystopian architectural projects of the preceding decade, in which architects experimented with self-sufficient models of cities that might become a reality after a nuclear catastrophe. At the same time, this kind of environment seems to anticipate one of the chief traits of the postmodern conception of space. Fredric Jameson elaborated on the nature of such a space in his seminal work *Post-Modernism, or, The Cultural Logic of Late Capitalism*, in which he analysed the lobby of John Portman's Westin Bonaventure Hotel in downtown Los Angeles: 'The Bonaventure aspired to being a total space, a complete world, a kind of miniature city ... Ideally, the minicity of Portman's Bonaventure ought not to have entrances at all, since the entryway is always the seam that links the building to the rest of the city that surrounds it; for it does not wish to be part of the city but rather its equivalent and replacement or substitute.'[4] Jameson obviously mourns the dramatic loss of public urban space in late capitalism. The total design of the environment in USM's advertising campaign does not share these broader cultural concerns, but illustrates how the notion of such completely autonomous and seemingly self-sufficient spaces has become a reality, or at least a very possible (and apparently desirable) future.

The theme of the hermetic self-referentiality of interior space continues in a USM ad for an office workspace from 1981. Here, the workspace is made up exclusively of the USM Haller system, and it is set in an entirely nondescript, seemingly endless interior without any clear differentiation between floor and walls. In comparison with similar advertising photographs from the 1960s, this workspace appears aseptic and clinically clean, and we wonder whether it has yet to be occupied. The most visible change in the setting, however, is the presence of a personal computer and its auxiliary hardware (such as keyboard and printer). The aesthetic of the technological equipment corresponds perfectly with the furniture's black-and-white surfaces, and the image strongly suggests that the USM Haller system is the perfect backdrop for the dawning digital age. Another advertising shoot from the following

4   Fredric Jameson, *Postmodernism, or, The Cultural Logic of Late Capitalism* (Durham, N.C.: Duke University Press, 2001), p. 40.

USM Haller, welcome desk, 1976

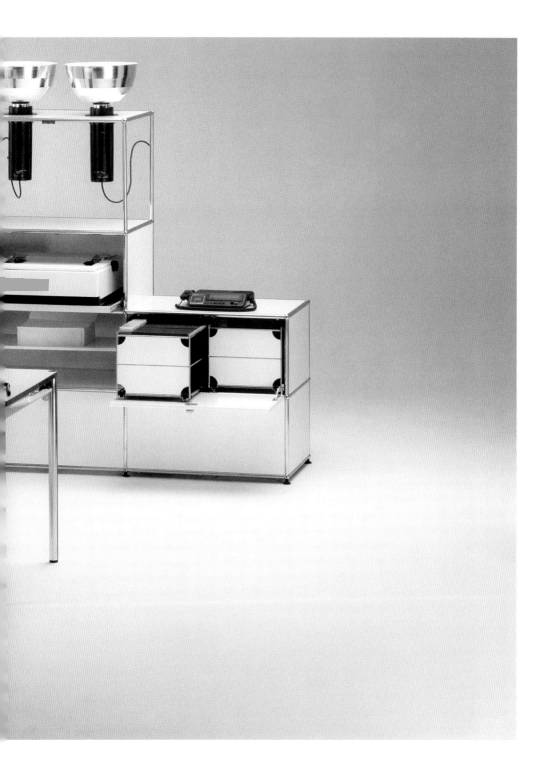

↑ USM Haller, open-plan architects' office, US, 1982

← ← USM Haller, single office workspace from the 1981 product catalogue

year presents the USM Haller system in a radically different light: we are looking into a busy office populated by a number of draughtsmen (most likely architects) in an artificially illuminated space submerged in warm colours. If in the year before the company had celebrated their product as a requisite for the future digital office space, it is now presented as offering a perfect backdrop and environment for creative professions. Almost all the surfaces, both vertical and horizontal, are covered with images, documents and tools, and the photograph suggests that it is the USM Haller system that helps to transform the flow of creative thinking into a structured process. Preceding the advent of computer-aided design, this image offers an alternative scenario to the futuristic computerized office space of the preceding year.

The last quarter of the 20th century saw the rise of what has become known as the 'star system' in architecture: buildings are commissioned and judged less for their spatial and social achievements than for the celebrity of their authors and their ability to present a particular architectural brand. (It should be added that these two aspects certainly do not exclude each other; however, the desired 'wow' factor has in many instances led to buildings that are proper works of art in themselves, but not necessarily adequate formal containers that best serve specific needs.) This shift in the public perception of architecture is reflected in USM's advertising campaigns as well, most notably a series of photographs featuring the furniture system in a residential and office building in Lugano designed by the Swiss architect Mario Botta. Not only does Botta belong to the first generation of 'star architects' that appeared from the 1980s onwards: his work also constitutes the Ticino School's most prominent contribution to postmodernism, being strongly rooted in the use of traditional building materials and in the architectural iconography of the region. In the USM advertising campaign, this is apparent in the use of stone for the exterior façade, the size and shape of the apertures, and the coffered vaulted ceiling. The architectural image conveyed here, deeply anchored in place and history, is a marked departure from the generic, universal spaces we have seen in the firm's advertisements up to this point. Once again, the USM Haller system adapts to this changed understanding of space elegantly and effortlessly. The 1960s aesthetic of modularity and technology has been transformed successfully into a classic icon of office furniture, something that is, like the architecture, both contemporary and historically conscious at the same time.

We find the USM Haller system juxtaposed with the dignifying architectural motif of the vault once again in a photograph that illustrates the Neue Messe exhibition centre in Leipzig. Here, however, the vault has monumental proportions and is made out of glass—clearly a reference to the Crystal Palace, the archetypal

USM Haller, units in an office building
by Mario Botta, Lugano, 1991

glass exhibition building designed by Joseph Paxton for the Great Exhibition of London in 1851. This ad for USM Haller, from 1995, adds yet another layer to how their furniture is conceived: situated at the image's vanishing point, and thus at its hub, the shelving unit being highlighted assumes the role of keystone in this visual— and, by extension, architectural—construction. It is as if the entire building rested on this piece of furniture and would collapse if it were taken away. The furniture seems to have merged completely with the architectural shell and to have become a quintessential element. But that is not all: framed by the arch, the USM Haller piece becomes the object of quasi-religious veneration. It takes on the meaning of an 'icon' and its connotations: a sacred, ritualistic object that is worshipped.[5] The USM Haller system has come a long way from its original conception as a universal way to arrange (corporate) space. Rather than just a system or a storage device for organizing the world of objects, it is an object in its own right, and a powerful one at that, captivating us with its presence.

One final example in this shifting landscape of meanings associated with USM is an advertisement from 2008 that presents a piece of furniture 'in private space'. Here, a low sideboard on the outdoor terrace of a home is set against the spectacular mountain scenery of Lake Lugano in southern Switzerland. The piece of furniture serves as both a framing device and a visual springboard for the natural scenery. It is both a luxurious item—a work of art, in fact—and a visual device that serves to pictorialize the natural backdrop. This is a far cry from what Fritz Haller had originally envisioned. The USM Haller system remains—formally and in terms of construction—remarkably unchanged. However, it is no longer appreciated simply as a functional device that fulfils certain needs, but as a precious aesthetic object in its own right.

5   See also Alina Payne, 'Architecture: Image, Icon or *Kunst der Zerstreuung?*', in Andreas Beyer, Matteo Burioni and Johannes Grave (eds), *Das Auge der Architektur: Zur Frage der Bildlichkeit in der Baukunst* (Munich: Wilhelm Fink, 2011), pp. 55–91; 59.

↑↑ USM Haller unit in the Neue Messe exhibition
centre, Leipzig, 1995

↑ USM Haller sideboard in a private interior
overlooking Lake Lugano, Switzerland, 2008

# REM KOOLHAAS

# HANS ULRICH OBRIST

# DYNAMIC
# LABYRINTH
# (SEOUL)

# Dynamic Labyrinth (Seoul)

## Rem Koolhaas
## Hans Ulrich Obrist

HANS ULRICH OBRIST    When was your first visit to Seoul?

REM KOOLHAAS    My first visit to Seoul was maybe six years
ago. We were working for Samsung, and it was a very interesting
experience because, in the first phase of the work, we were working
with a Chaebol (a conglomerate of many companies) at its most
megalomaniac, really insanely megalomaniac. I think at that point,
they were doing six hundred architectural projects, and this meant
that there was an incredible traffic of international architects there
who did not know of [one] another—that they were there, that they
were working for the same client, what they were doing. So it
was a typically unpleasant sort of architectural competition. And
we were always surrounded by these kinds of phalanxes of some
sort of executive assistants, etc. And the funniest thing is that we
were doing a sort of museum, with Mario Botta, Jean Nouvel, and
ourselves, which was a combination that had not been engineered
by ourselves but engineered by someone near the chairman and his
wife took a particular interest in it, and at some point, I needed to
explain the project to the chairman, and I was waiting in the Shilla
Hotel, which is an incredible hotel—the level of smoothness
in it is really unbelievable, it's as if you're in a dream in terms of
preemptive service and preemptive comfort. But anyway, I was
waiting, and then suddenly at four o'clock in the morning, there
was banging on my door, and it was the same Samsung executives,

who said, 'You have to see the chairman now.' And I said, 'Why at this time?' It was the first meeting. And they said, 'You have to see him now because he will be arrested at nine o'clock in the morning!' So I went, and I saw the chairman between six and eight. It was very quiet. He disclosed the whole thing; but that was also, of course, the first signal that things were going to change there. It was in a way the beginning of the crisis, when all of the endemic corruption was kind of dealt with, which showed the fragility of the whole economic structure and then its unravelling. So we made this project—it was actually a very interesting project. We had to connect the different architectures of Jean Nouvel and Mario Botta, who had started it. Our project is mostly underground. It is two volumes, on a very beautiful hill, one of those parks full of villas. And because we did not want to add another building, we made a straight slice horizontally, part of which goes into the mountain and part of which emerges from the mountain, so that many of the facilities are underground. It was an interesting project. It's also a museum and cultural institution. The only mark we've left so far in Seoul is a kind of enormous underground pit dug into granite. It is in a way the most beautiful building. And what I tried to convince them, is to leave the pit, to do something with that incredibly bare … it's just the biggest negative space you've ever seen.

HUO   Can you tell me what it is that you particularly like about Seoul?

RK   What I think is really beautiful about Seoul is that it is a city that occurred on a site where there cannot really be a city. There isn't really room for a city there. So it's as if the metropolis has been established in the middle of the mountains, a city that has to coexist with mountains and beautiful forests, a kind of 'Manhattan in the Alps'. The middle class lives in the flat parts, those who can afford everything and those who can't afford anything live on the hills. And throughout the city are scattered the remnants of this Metabolist project. And I simply like the speed with which it expands. I think Korean people are the most direct in Asia; they are very raw and direct, not prisoners of politeness, and very humorous.

HUO   What about the screens? Do you like those big screens?

RK   I think the screens are beautiful from a distance. From the hills, you see these flickering screens.

HUO   You mentioned that when you visited Seoul for the first time after the economic crisis, it was all of a sudden a completely different city. The city completely changed in a few days …

OMA, Leeum Museum,
Seoul, 2004

RK   Yes, in a way, the future seems to be telescoping, and this exacerbates the inability I've always had to conceptualize the future as future. The future is telescoping to the point that not only can you no longer predict ten years or five years ahead but the acceleration of everything seems to make even next month completely inscrutable and unpredictable. And one of the strongest signs of this kind of acceleration is in the Asian crisis, and how the Asian crisis has had an immediate impact on urban conditions— which sometimes had only existed for three years, but in those three years, there were brand new sparkling products of the Asian economic miracle. Soaring cities, exploding cities, then all of a sudden ... Then, while everyone here was writing about the collapse, there was already a kind of resurgence, and now the apparent gain in strength. And this whole cycle was in a way a total mystery to people in the West because nobody here grasped the speed of it, nor can anybody explain why it happened. My theory is that China saved the capitalist world by not going bankrupt and by not devaluing its currency, and that the Communist system in the end, in a very paradoxical way, came to the rescue of the capitalist system. That is something you never read about. And my most perfect demonstration of it is that Seoul—a city known for its eternal traffic—in the middle of the crisis, all of a sudden became this kind of eerie, silent city with no traffic: a city without pollution. And maybe that was when I could finally see that Seoul was a kind of Switzerland, really beautiful.

HUO   In previous interviews and texts, you always said that you despised futuristic city predictions; you said that you preferred to talk about present conditions.

RK   I think anyone in their right mind should simply give it up. All you can hope for today is some kind of intelligence about day-to-day decisions. Another example, which is not as extreme as Asia, is that we've been involved in Seattle for maybe a year, and that within that year, there have been major upheavals happening in the city that made it defenceless. From a kind of perfect city without any trouble, it turned into a troubled, anxious city: there were also the first major anti-capitalist demonstrations since the New Deal, which traumatized the entire administration, and the fact that Microsoft, even nine months ago, was a completely vigorous, powerful, monopolistic entity that is now condemned and about to be divided, and Bill Gates, once a complete myth, now is no longer CEO, but chairman, etc. All those things are an incredible demonstration of how there is absolutely no certainty that you can count on. And the interesting thing is that the clients are trying to outwit this situation by increasingly accelerating the whole pace of architecture. The buildings we once had to build in two years we now have to build in one year. In that sense, it was a good instinct to document in our Harvard research, in general, how fast architecture can be produced. But I could never have imagined at that time, when I discovered that some buildings in Shenzhen were produced in two afternoons on a home computer, that two or three years later we would be in the same position. But we are. And even so, we realize that we are not quick enough, or that architecture can never be quick enough.

OMA, 'La Défense Masterplan', competition entry, Paris, 2008

HUO     Does this affect the life span of buildings?

RK     This is really interesting actually. There is this planning project for La Defense Paris we did, where we considered everything more than 25 years old theoretically obsolete, ready to be taken down, so that you could build a new city on the site of the old. At the time, it was considered totally visionary and an outrage. I recently had to give a presentation for the station in Rotterdam, where there will be a super fast TGV train, and again I launched the suggestion that after 25 years you could simply declare buildings redundant because they are so mediocre, and this time, there was a sort of barely suppressed nervous laughter. This limited life span of buildings is still an absolute area of blindness and real taboo in Europe.

HUO     And in America?

RK     In America, you can only say in retrospect that in many cases this is true, but you can never make it the basis of architectural

OMA, 'La Défense Masterplan', competition entry, Paris, 2008

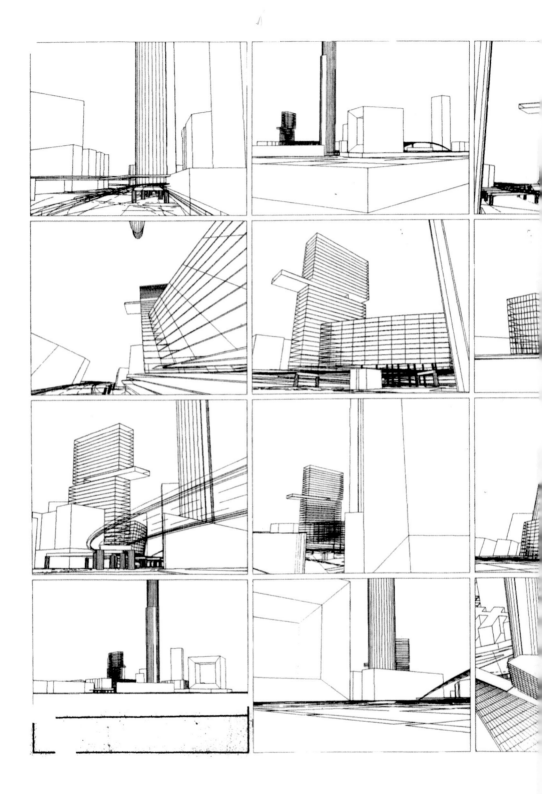

OMA, 'La Défense Masterplan',
competition entry, Paris, 2008

196    The Modular

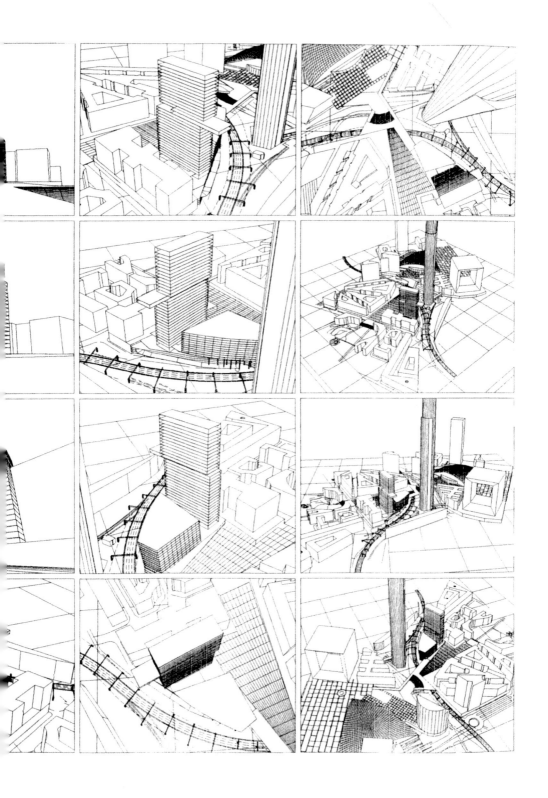

production in the beginning. And this is really unfortunate because I think it could liberate an enormous amount of energy if you could be more independent vis-à-vis the lifetime of a building, and, by implication, the context. Nevertheless, we are of course contradicting ourselves when we do a public building, and we do not design it as if it will disappear in 25 years. But the pressure would be less if it were an automatic given that a building will exist 25 years at the most.

HUO    What is the part between slowness and speed?

RK    It remains a very strong tension. In that sense, it is a very fascinating thing to see this medium—architecture—that is now so popular but has a sort of inherent resistance to completely following the current tendency, which is toward acceleration. It may be that that is a real conundrum for architecture, that it can accelerate, but that it also has some kind of intimate resistance, maybe more than television, film, or music, and maybe that is why it is so interesting today. But it also means that we have now discovered that architecture can never reach certain speeds, and that discovery pushes us into another domain, where the same kind of thinking now has to be applied in a much more conceptual, theoretical, and disembodied way.

HUO    You mentioned OMA's library project for Seattle (Seattle Public Library, 2004). I think there is a certain relationship between the notion of the museum and the notion of the library, both often very defensive institutions, and moralistic, too. Energizing these institutions evokes examples from the 1960s, for instance, Cedric Price's Fun Palace (1960–1964), or the way Willem Sandberg ran the Stedelijk Museum in Amsterdam. Is this part of your personal history as well?

RK    The moment I discovered art as an independent person, as a teenager basically, coincided with the Sandberg regime. The exhibition designs completely changed the museum each time. 'Dylaby— a Dynamic Labyrinth,' (Stedelijk Museum, Amsterdam, 1962) would now be a prophetic title again. All those shows were the kind of shows that enabled me to be more modern than my parents... So in a way, I was kind of indoctrinated by it. And I think all of that had a big influence on my museum projects. But of course, at the same time, the museum, even in the 1960s, was a very demanding place, in the sense that it insisted on participation and was presenting issues fairly aggressively. The big difference between now and the 1960s is not only that this kind of aggression or those demands are missing in the presentations, but I think the sheer numbers are drastically changing the entire equation, limiting

↑ OMA, Seattle Central Library, 2004

→→ OMA, Seattle Central Library, 2004

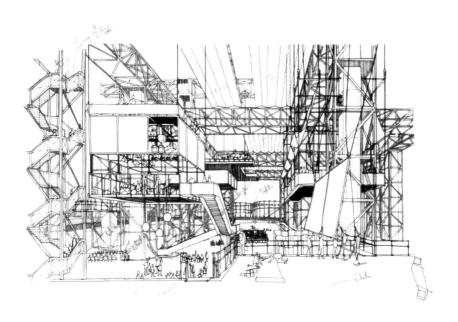

Cedric Price, 'Fun Palace', 1960–64

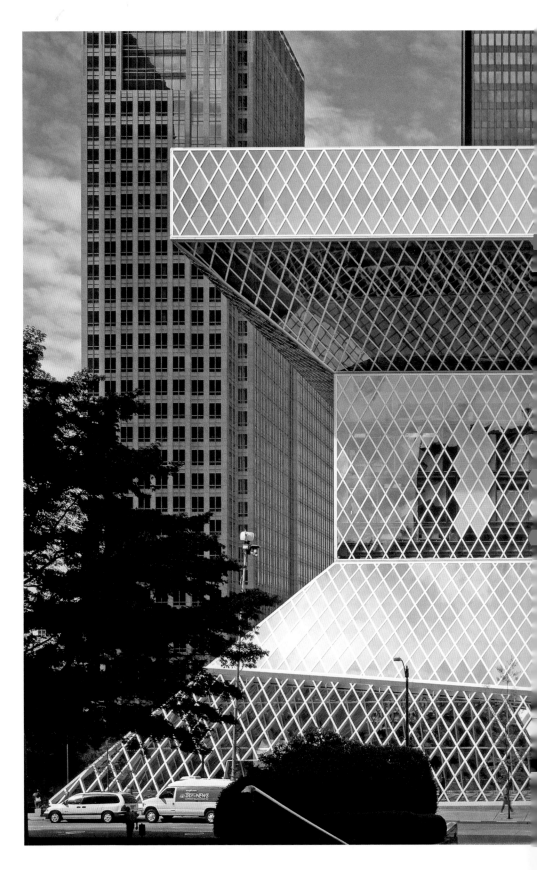

the things you can say and do in a museum. One of the things no curator liked about our designs for the Tate or the MoMA [Museum of Modern Art, New York] was the notion of creating a fast-track tourist trajectory, a kind of shortcut that would also enable the return of slowness, or intensity. In the absence of a two-speed system, the museum experience is accelerated for everybody, you can see it with the new Tate installations, not based on accumulations but on 'juxtaposition'—the grids by Gilbert & George next to Mondrian, a quick 'Aha!' and on to the next 'rhyme,' all a form of fast-track, against complexity.

I think this is equally true for the library. Apart from all the kinds of ideologies that you could have—or launch or repeat or renew—the sheer fact of the numbers needs to be incorporated within the concept or course of each of these projects. You are often referring to the beautiful era of MoMa, 'the Laboratory years,'—and it *was* a beautiful era, but I don't think that you can have a laboratory visited by two million people a year. And that is why both our libraries and our museums are trying to organize the coexistence of urban noise experiences and experiences that enable focus and slowness. That is, for me, the most exciting way of thinking today—the incredible surrender to frivolity and how it could also be compatible with a seduction of focus and stillness. The issues of masses of visitors and the core experience of stillness and being together with the work are what is at issue in the [Seattle] project.

HUO   Richard Hamilton recently made a text piece in the form of a badge with the text 'Give me hard copy.' It's actually a fragment that he extracted from Ridley Scott's move Blade Runner (1982). Accordingly, the idea is that the museum gives the hard copy and the library does, too. So I was wondering how you see the role of the museum and the library in terms of network conditions. How do you see the relation between the actual and the virtual? How do you avoid having hierarchies between different actual libraries and virtual libraries?

RK   I think this is very interesting because in Seattle, there is a library system made up of 24 libraries, and this is the main library. So this is already a sort of hierarchical position in itself, which assumes that the main body of the government is in the main library. And so there is all the history and routine of centralism. But of course, it is entirely networked and about to be more networked. And what I find fascinating is that there is a lot of work going on these days by people like Judith Donath at MIT (Massachusetts Institute of Technology), who are looking at the Internet but also at different kinds of databases as potential sources to fabricate new communities. And the irony is that, on the basis

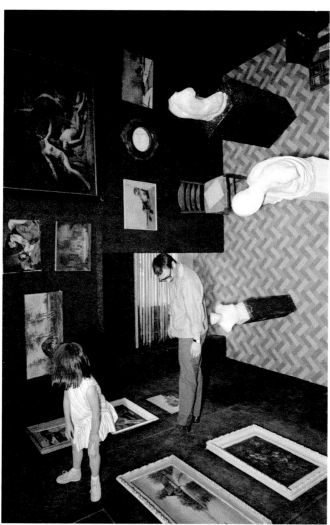

← *Dylaby—
a Dynamic
Labyrinth*, exhibition
view, Stedelijk
Museum,
Amsterdam, 1962

↓ Martial Raysse,
'Raysse Beach',
exhibition view,
Stedelijk Museum,
Amsterdam, 1962

of network conditions, which are always assumed to be increasingly democratic, you can, of course, create new hierarchies. And currently the latent and almost threshold question is: 'Does a network imply homogeneity?' or 'Does a network imply democracy?' or 'Does a network imply privacy?' the discourse on networks has always been a disturbance to universal distribution, but I don't see any ultimate reason why that should be the case, why its opposite potential should not be investigated. The moment at which the library will be able to connect, for instance, all the data that the readers generate—who reads which books—then that would be an incredible way of modernizing their function.

HUO    At which point the library becomes an agent, to guide people on what to read...

RK    Yes, but there is the question of privacy. And the same for the museum. And that is why I said yesterday that it's not only the end of the future but also the end of privacy. There's a whole thing, like a reservoir; you feel that the wall is cracking and that you'll simply go. And about the issue of flattening and hierarchy or value, the Internet does not only have to flatten value, it can also be used to create value because you can disseminate eighty percent, and make the next ten percent really difficult, and the next five percent even more difficult, and then have a core two percent, which represents the equivalent of rare books: the rare information.

HUO    What exactly do you set against flattening?

RK    Instead of flattening, you can create value. And the defen-siveness is not only in the wardens, it is also in the repulsive domain of public art, which so rarely is anything but the nostalgic reinforcement of, or compensation for, an abandoned domain, and therefore rarely able to convince anyone but itself. And if you ask about aging cities, the context of the city is no longer a physical context. And still, when we talk and think about context, we routinely think about mass.

HUO    Reading will be one function among other functions?

RK    Yes, even if it's not really an interference. Since reading is only one of the advances in the library, we hope that what we are doing is creating space where advances can take place. We've always done that. We've always noticed that, when the chips are down, there is nobody to run those kinds of programs, nobody to conceptualize that kind of activity, even though the buildings themselves would support it incredibly well. That is why we are very vehement that it's very important that somebody take care of that kind of thinking. But the tragedy is that in libraries, there is still such an incredible war between words and images, even if in the outside world, it's completely gone.

HUO    I was wondering if you could tell me more about these different platforms. It's a very Deleuzian idea, a mille plateaux idea because they're really high-connectivity platforms.

RK    Because the departments are very specific, we need to address their specificity in a precise way. But of course, we also hope that more will happen than is defined in the program, so between platforms are the public spaces that, less contained, have room to evolve. In civil architecture, like in physics, the pressure between two dense plates in itself can create an enormous tension, and programming those plates can also trigger events in-between. We try to make the floor and the ceiling interactive, so that you could see clouds of colour but also clouds of information. An aesthetic spectacle, so you could basically summon the people to come together at a certain point, or scatter them in different directions. So in that sense, we are becoming more ambitious about recording those problems in the architecture, too.

HUO    Does this mean that the different sections will not become ghettos, but that there will be interdisciplinary exchange?

RK    The whole thing was about breaking up this kind of division into departments, where one floor is this, another floor is that. We are reorganizing all that.

HUO    But you still have four main sections?

RK    Not really 'main.' It has become a continuous spiral of subjects, and there is a journey through it. It's not really a subdivision, in my view, it's more what the French call a *mise en relation*, which doesn't exist in English, or perhaps you could translate it as 'continuous exposure.'

HUO    This interview started with the city, then we came to Seattle—the library, specifically: you talked about connectivity, hyper-connectivity within the building. In my last interview with Peter Smithson, I asked him about how he sees the present condition of the city. Here is what he answered: 'I think that the critical thing to work through now is the space between. Most of the world out there is a nightmare. I worked in Montreal last winter, and the drive from the international airport to the city

was one factory after another, one group of dwellings … it is unbelievable. And it has happened so fast: in twenty years, a generation
has almost wiped out the notion of architecture … But there is no
sense of the collective, the space between: all buildings are built

Alison and Peter
Smithson, 'Escalator
system for Berlin',
1958

as if they existed only in themselves.' Do you share this view? Isn't
it true also for Holland?

RK   We see that there is an incredible dysfunctionality in terms
of connections. We are really interested in working and thinking
on the meta-structural or infrastructural level on concepts to
improve conditions. Last night, it took Fernando Romero two
and a half hours to get from Rotterdam to Amsterdam by public
transportation, by train. He did all the socially right things:
he walked to the station, took the train and the tram. So there
is this kind of insanity in which, if you take public means of
transportation in the way that you're intended to do, it takes three
times as long as going by car. That's why everyone takes their
car, and that's why the car doesn't work either. It's a vicious circle.
And we are incredibly interested in it and (we're) also good at
conceptualizing interventions and solutions, but the difficulty is
that that is the level of politics, and that is the level that is the
hardest to ever enter. And even if you enter, you're going to be
typecast very quickly as either a visionary, who has interesting
but irrelevant visions, or a nuisance … or a megalomaniac. I think
there is something touching about Smithson and Team 10: they
were obsessed with conceptualizing new types and families
of connections. And my feeling about their residue, their effect,
is both more cynical and more optimistic because I think, to
a large extent, things connect in spite of the efforts of the architect.
There is an incredible infrastructure or architecture of connection,

particularly in this century: all the ramps, all the highway crossings, all the pedestrian connections, etc.; and my instinctive belief is that they all hinder exactly the kind of communication that they are supposed to generate. In Lagos, connections proliferate in spite of the infrastructure, or of the dead-end, the fiasco of infrastructure. That is typically one of the aspects of the profession that is fighting a rearguard action because it denies all the connections that are already in place, already in supposedly lost or residual space. And for me, the fact that those autonomous parts can exist now because there are remnants of invisible connections, is for me the interesting point, that somehow, those invisible connections need an architecture, and that that kind of architecture probably benefits from a relationship with real architecture. And so that is why we are interested in that kind of virtual reality because it enables you to conceptualize something without being literate about computer use or computer animation.

HUO    Can you tell me about your interdisciplinary project at Harvard University, the Harvard Design School Project on the city?

RK    Harvard is a school of architecture, a school of landscape, and a school of planning, where smart and more or less autonomous and independent people are both teachers and students. And the interesting thing is that these groups have the say to appoint new people, so on the whole, they're always appointed in conformity with what these fields represent. Architecture has lost certain abilities; landscape has taken them over. What could be very interesting is to unite these residues, and what we have called it is this fourth thing. It is more a thing than a space, and to declare that this is the perfect domain to participation in a redefinition of ... if within a school like Harvard you made a consultation of all the marginal people, you would obviously have some kind of government in exile, a kind of exiled Harvard, but also—and that would be more and more obvious—you would find that all those people have some intelligence that can no longer fit completely into a given mould. So it's not really interdisciplinarity *per se*, but more about the power of marginalizing.

# GO
# HASEGAWA

# I TRY TO BE
# ARCHITECTURE

# I Try To Be Architecture

## Interview with Go Hasegawa
## and Sho Kurokawa

I

INTERVIEWER   If we define architecture primarily as the production of confined spaces, how should we understand your house design called 'Pilotis in a Forest' or a traditional house in Kyodo?

GO HASEGAWA   For me, we must always have an architectural element, like a roof or pilotis, in mind. Architectural elements represent a kind of wisdom and knowledge, as people have used them for a long time. It is wisdom and knowledge that enable the creation of a space. I like to start from that idea, because everybody is familiar with it and, as an architect, I can use it to communicate and be close to people. At the same time I always try to expand our physical sensations through the choice of certain architectural elements. In architecture, it is very important to have both the feeling of being protected and an openness towards the outside world at the same time. Some architectural elements can do both. So I start by reacting to the environment and observing our feelings towards it—as with 'Pilotis in a Forest'. I try to make buildings that reference traditional architecture but at the same time will be somehow new.

Go Hasegawa, 'House in Kyodo', Tokyo, 2011

Go Hasegawa's masterclass at work, Domaine de Boisbuchet, France, 2014

Those traditional elements that have been used for hundreds of years, could you think of them as a kind of module?

GH    Yes. They're a kind of module, a kind of tool. Modules are not only system-based units, such as panels or bricks: they are also architectural components like the ones I just mentioned. Modules enable us to make comparisons with other buildings. I want to make buildings that allow people to think. This is very important for architecture.

When you use older elements in your architecture, how do you achieve innovation?

GH    I think architects should aim to offer a new physical sensation. It is essential to create interior spaces, but I also believe that architecture in particular can be a tool for expanding the body's sense of the exterior. Using new proportions for individual parts can help a lot: we can uncover new ideas of the traditional through proportion. I always try to find new proportions for these architectural elements, such as pilotis 6.5 metres [21 feet] high or a roof 6 centimetres [2 3/8 inches] thick.

↑ Go Hasegawa, 'Pilotis in a Forest', Gunma, Japan, 2010

→ Go Hasegawa, 'House in Gotanda', Tokyo, 2006

Your practice is oriented towards pre-existing elements. Are there also components in your architecture that you invent from scratch?

GH   Of course, I think my buildings are very different from their neighbours: I give spaces a new feel. At the same time we cannot communicate with each other properly without having some similarities. So existing buildings, their proportions and their elements can be a kind of model. Perhaps I view the neighbours' building as a model for my own, yes. Of course, there are some architects who build completely differently from others. I don't like those projects, even if they're beautiful, because they ignore the environment and local ways of constructing.

This relationship with the outside world that you create through your architecture, how does it work? Does it result from a kind of a transparency or from something else?

GH   Yes, it is a kind of transparency, but the not
visual kind you have with a glass box. Instead I try
to create a sense of continuity between the interior
and the exterior by using new proportions. I think
it's freer than visual transparency. *Espèces d'espaces*
['Species of Spaces', 1974] by Georges Perec is one
of my favourite books. He wrote about various kinds
of spaces but at the same time lets us think about
the boundaries in between. What is the boundary
between a room and an apartment? Between
an apartment and the street? All kinds of spaces
are created by human beings, but nowadays our
experience is too strongly defined by functional
classifications of space. It would be very bad if we
lost our freedom because we can conceive of a space
only functionally. In my work I try to reconsider
and to overcome these classifications.

> The idea of creating a space that makes you feel
> protected from the outside but at the same time
> encourages a connection with the outside sounds
> interesting.

Go Hasegawa,
'House in
Gotanda',
Tokyo, 2006

GH    Yes. It might be strange to put it like this, but with every project I try to imagine how the building itself might feel. I don't just think about how the client will feel inside the space. I always try to 'be' the architecture. I believe that the coexistence of a human scale and the building's scale gives us freedom. People can sense a kind of scale of that relates to living, but at the same time they can connect directly with the outside through the building's scale. The big door I designed for a house in Gotanda, Tokyo, is a good example.

When you think as if you were an element of architecture, what feeling are you searching for?

GH    Very comfortable, very private but at that same time open towards the world at large. As one of the 'rethink the modular' curators said, it's very important to have two opposite concepts in one space. It's a contradiction, but we can make it possible through proportion and the scale.

When you spoke about transparency, were you referring to modernism, which is perhaps a very European concept? Or do you look to Japanese archetypes to provide modules for your architecture?

GH    Our generation is influenced by both European and Japanese architecture. For example, Toyo Ito's generation tries to overcome European modernism, and they have tried to overcome the legacy of Le Corbusier and Mies van der Rohe. The Japanese architect Kazuyo Sejima is an incredibly important figure for us. Thanks to her and her generation, we can view Japanese contemporary architecture and European modernism on an equal footing. Why do we all have to think about ways of replacing modernism? This is how our generation feels. We can use what we learned from modernism and also continue the achievements of Sejima's generation. I can use anything architects have ever made anywhere: nowadays we don't need an enemy in order to create architecture. This might be a tendency of my generation in Japan. History can be a useful tool for making something new but also maintaining a certain continuity.

I was intrigued when I saw the large number of models in your office. How much do you work with maquettes to develop new proportions in your buildings?

GH   We always make a lot of models and compare them with each other. Of course, we have an idea and then we make a model, but sometimes models make us think further. So models are not just for checking out our ideas or recording our designs. It's always the models that bring us to a place we had never thought of. The architect and the model can disagree. It's a very interesting and exciting moment for me. I don't like remaining stationary. I'm afraid of doing just what we already know.

How do you perceive the landscape and spatial qualities of this very rural area of France, the Domaine de Boisbuchet, where you led your USM masterclass?

GH   I worry a little if we can recognize it only as a beautiful landscape. It's not precise, it's too rough. We might forget how to understand the beauty of the landscape. We live in very functional, limited spaces —that's why we lost sight of how to enjoy landscapes. People who lived maybe one thousand years ago must have had a more developed sense of the landscape to feel something special in this environment. I asked my students, 'What do you think of it?' They said, 'Yeah, it's beautiful. It's amazing.' But I have a hypothesis that the landscape around Boisbuchet is more than beautiful, more than amazing. Some-how I'd like to find a new kind of conception of the spaces contained within this beautiful environment. This is the first time I've thought like this, and it's very exciting!

II                Sho Kurokawa, how did you come to dig that extraordinary hole during your masterclass with Go Hasegawa, and how did it relate to the theme of modularity?

SHO KUROKAWA   It is still really hard to tell you how we came to the decision to dig, but we were digging there and we just dug a very primitive hole. We went to Boisbuchet without preparing anything

↑↑ Go Hasegawa's masterclass, 'Hole',
Domaine de Boisbuchet, France, 2014

↑ Go Hasegawa's masterclass, 'Column',
Milan, 2015

beforehand. We decided things on site, and resources there were quite limited, so we decided to use our bodies because we wanted something specific to the group. We took the simple, primitive gesture of digging and we learned from that. We did a similar thing for the exhibition in Milan. We then said, 'Let's find the modular, let's find that kind of structure by ourselves in the environment.' This hole, then, has quite a complex story behind it—one that involves human scale, the scale of collectiveness, the scale of the environment and the context of place, especially the particular place surrounding Boisbuchet. We also thought a lot about hidden scales, about modularity hidden within the environment.

So, as it turns out, even the placement of the hole in a big field outside the château is quite deliberate, isn't it? It's not a randomly placed hole at all.

SK    No. We tried to perceive and structure the environment in new ways, so its location could not be really casual or random. In order to observe elements of the scenery in the way we wanted to, we needed to be at that precise spot. The hole, for example, is more or less 75 centimetres [30 inches] deep. When we sat on the floor within the hole, our eyes were level with the grass. From that eye level, the depth of field, the depth of scenery was in effect cancelled out. We started to see single elements within the landscape, one detached from another. They're not really structured or composed. We began to see the singularity of the château, a tree, our shed, our dormitory space. The view from the hole enabled a non-hierarchical perception of the things around us. That's what we wanted to produce as a space.

That was the project you worked on during your masterclass. But how does what we can see exhibited here in Milan relate to what you did back there? In your case, there's a radical change of direction. Tell us about the column of rope.

SK    For us, in fact, there's no change of direction. It forms part of a series of investigations. One was the hole in Boisbuchet, and the second was the column in Milan. The connection is how we can learn from the earth, the soil. In Boisbuchet we performed an intervention in the soil. Here we used earth from Milan, from Lorenzo Bini's construction site, and we measured this environment through the creation of a column. In France, we respected the height of our eye level. Here, in order to work on a human scale we took the measurement of a cross-section of rope. It measured 4 centimetres [1½ inches] across, which is quite a comfortable dimension to put your hand around. The rope could not be thinner and could not be much bigger. So that's the link with the scale of the body. In Boisbuchet, we decided on the hole's dimensions by joining hands, meaning that it related precisely to our team, to the seven of us who were present. The diameter of the column here in Milan is 56 centimetres [22 inches], which was the size of the circle made when our team sat back-to-back together. That's the size of the column we wanted to lean on. It adds the collective dimension that was present in the hole. The column is obviously the most important element for defining the space of the Salone dei Tessuti in Milan. In fact, the column's overall dimensions were determined by the length of the rope. It measures 113 metres (371 feet) long, which is a very important dimension for modern cities: the famous grid developed by Cerdà for Barcelona in the middle of the 19th century uses the same length. This neighbourhood in Milan, which was developed in the early 19th century, seems to be based on a similar system. This street, Via San Gregorio, has nearly exactly the same dimensions. We transformed this measurement of length found in the surrounding urban context into a measurement of height, resulting in a 2.1-metre column. It represents a connection between the city, our bodies, the group and the exhibition hall.

Go Hasegawa, one of the tutors of seven USM masterclasses, was interviewed during the 'rethink the modular' workshop at the Domaine de Boisbuchet, France, 2014 (I). Sho Kurokawa was a participant in the masterclass and was interviewed as a spokesperson for the team on the occasion of the 'rethink the modular' exhibition in Milan, 2015 (II).

# ALVA NOË

# WIDE MINDS

# Wide Minds

## Alva Noë

We know better now. We know that that life of man whose
unfolding furnishes psychology its material is the most
difficult and complicated subject which man can investigate.
We have some consciousness of its ramifications and of its
connections. We see that man is somewhat more than a neatly
dovetailed psychical machine who may be taken as an isolated
individual, laid on the dissecting table of analysis and duly
anatomized. We know that his life is bound up with the life
of society, of the nation in the ethos and nomos; we know
that he is closely connected with all the past by the lines
of education, tradition, and heredity; we know that man
is indeed the microcosm who has gathered into himself
the riches of the world, both of space and of time, the world
physical and the world psychical.

– John Dewey

[...] I [have previously] offered evidence that the brain gives rise
to consciousness by enabling an exchange between the person or
animal and the world. What emerges from this discussion is a new
conception of ourselves as expanded, extended, and dynamic. In
this chapter I place this discovery in a larger context. Our bodies
and our minds are active. By changing the shape of our activity, we

can change our own shape, body, and mind. Language, tools, and collective practices make us what we are. Where do you stop, and where does the rest of the world begin? There is no reason to suppose that the critical boundary is found in our brains or our skin.

## WHERE DO WE FIND OURSELVES?

We now think of economies as globalized, corporations as internationalized, information networks as distributed. We ourselves are also dynamically distributed, boundary crossing, offloaded, and environmentally situated, by our very nature. What explains our inability until now to understand consciousness is that we've been searching for it in the wrong place.

I remember vividly one day in the 1970s—I must have been eleven or twelve—when my father addressed me sharply on the street in front of our building in New York: "Stop acting that way immediately. You're behaving like ..." He paused to find the right word. "You're behaving like an American!" I don't recall what I was doing. Perhaps I was singing aloud or doing a little dance step, or in some other way carrying on in public. My father was an immigrant who'd arrived in New York at the end of 1949, having made it through the clutches of the Nazis and the Soviets; he was grateful to America—convinced he would not have survived for their intervention in the war—and glad to enjoy the freedom and anonymity of New York City. But a part of him, at least sometimes—so I was startled to discover—was anything but at home here. America, for my father, was brash, unmannered, loud, superficial, and above all foreign. Although he loved me, at that moment, at least, he was revolted—I don't think that is too strong a word—by his very own son for being what he— that is, what I—could not help being: a native of this new place.

I've since learned that this is a very common bind for immigrants. It is usually hardship that forces them to seek a home in a strange land. But what struck me—and I think I appreciated this even as a child, in the face of my father's displeasure—was the thought that he was divided against himself. The revulsion he felt toward me and toward the place where he found himself showed just how displaced and indeed, in a way, disfigured he was.

This is a [text] about consciousness, about the human mind and the project of understanding it as belonging to our biological natures. It is not a memoir or a tale of my father's immigration. I mention this personal anecdote because it underscores an important idea—and also because my own preoccupation with this problem may have had its beginnings in this early experience. What my father's plight illustrates is that, at a very basic level, we are involved—that is to say, tangled up—with the places we find ourselves. We are of them. A person is not a selfcontained module or autonomous whole. We are not like the berry that can be easily plucked, but rather like the plant itself, rooted in the earth and enmeshed in the brambles. When we transplant ourselves as immigrants get transplanted, when we move from one town to another or one country to another, we suffer injury, however subtly or grotesquely or even painlessly, and so we are altered. This should not come as a surprise. Our life is a flow of activity, and it depends on our possession of habits and skills and practical knowledge whose very actuality in turn implicates our particular niches. No matter how good you are at breathing, you can't breathe underwater, just as you can't swim where there is no water. And no matter how charming you may be, how wonderful a raconteur, if you find yourself in a strange land where a strange language is spoken, you can't tell a good story—that is, you can't be what you are. You yourself are changed.

Where do you stop, and where does the rest of the world begin? The blithe confidence of the neuroscientist that the brain is the seat of consciousness amounts to an unearned conviction that we can draw the boundary between ourselves and the rest of the world at the skull. For some purposes that may be a good way to go. If you want to know how many people are in attendance at the ball game, don't count the number of arms: count heads. But counting depends on settled ways of individuating that which we wish to count. It is a highly purpose-relative activity. Are the dandelions in the meadow one plant, joined as they are through a common root system, or many? Is the Macintosh OS one program, the operating system, or is it many: a mail program, a calendar program, etc.? Is Williams-Sonoma one company or many? How we draw these lines usually depends on what we are interested in. Are we programmers or potential investors? Do we work for the antitrust division of the Justice Department? It also depends on what we want to accomplish. One of the central claims of this [text] is that if we seek to understand human or animal consciousness, then we ought to focus not on the brain alone but on the brain in context—that is, on the brain in the natural setting of the active life of the person or animal. For what we bearers of consciousness are—as the example of my father serves to illustrate—depends on where we are and what we can do.

## MAGICAL BOUNDARIES AND THE RUBBER-HAND ILLUSION

Where do you stop, and where does the rest of the world begin? One extreme view would have it that you are your brain: you stop at its limits. The skull, roughly, is the boundary of yourself. You may think that the pain of stubbing your toe is in your toe and that the feeling of the glass is in your hand, but you are mistaken. The feeling itself is not in your hand or toe; it is in your brain. Granted, it is the action of the cup on the sensory fibers in your hand, or the activation of nerve endings in your toe, that causes the neural activation in your head in which your feeling consists. But you'd have the feeling even if there were no cup or no foot, just so long as the right pattern of activation was brought about. The real sensation is in your head, not in your body. Something vaguely like this idea may inform people who say that the brain is the most important erogenous zone.

This claim is yet another version of the prevalent neuroscientific dogma that you are your brain and that all the rest—the sense of our emplacement in a world that is meaningful and populated by others—is a myth promulgated for us by our brains. However intoxicating it might be to think that science has this to teach us—"we live behind a veil of illusion"—there is no reason to be convinced. The established facts are only these: sensation requires the action of the nervous system; there is no human or animal life without a nervous system. But from this it does not follow either that the nervous system is alone sufficient for sensation or that our selves are confined to our brains and nerve tissue.

The rubber-hand illusion, as it is sometimes called, provides a lovely piece of support for what I am claiming. This demonstration, first performed by Matthew Botvinick and Jonathan Cohen and reported in the journal *Nature* in 1998—in an article entitled "Rubber Hand Feels Touch That Eyes See"—is a stunning illustration of the fact that the sense of where we are is shaped dynamically by our interaction with the environment in multiple sensory modalities.

The demonstration went like this (I simplify only slightly): You are asked to sit at a table. Your right hand is on your lap and is concealed from your view by the table. Across the table rests a rubber hand, the sort of thing you might find in a shop selling scary toys for Halloween. You watch as a person gently taps and strokes the rubber hand with a delicate paintbrush. Tap tap, stroke stroke, tap stroke, stroke stroke stroke tap. In perfect synchrony, an experimenter is tapping your actual right hand out of view underneath the table. Now something remarkable happens. You have the very distinct feeling that you are being touched on the rubber hand: that the feeling of being touched that is, in fact, occurring on your own, connected right hand under the table is taking place on the rubber hand across the table! As the article's title suggests, you feel the touching of the rubber hand that the eyes see. If you are asked to point with your left hand, which is also under the table, to the place where you feel yourself being touched, you will point (roughly) in the direction of the rubber hand.

This is an example of a very striking and prevalent phenomenon: the power of what we see to influence our nonvisual sensory experience. This is known in psychology as visual capture. It is the phenomenon that underlies ventriloquism. What causes you to hear the words coming from the mouth of the dummy is the fact that you see the dummy's mouth opening and closing in sync with the words themselves. You hear what you see. This is a robust effect; we experience it when we go to the movies, where the actor imaged on the screen seems to be producing the sounds. In fact, the sounds emanate from speakers that are located elsewhere in the room. In one important study, speakers play two distinct unrelated streams of speech, creating a jumble of speech noise. You can't understand either stream until you are given visual cues in the form of video images of the faces doing the talking. The spatial distinctness of the visually apparent sources of the sounds enables you to discern the distinct streams of speech when you were unable to do this otherwise.

In fact, visual capture—the powerful influence of vision on other sensory modalities—is an important element in normal, true speech perception. We unconsciously read lips when we are engaged in conversation, and what we hear—what sounds we take in—depends critically on what we see. To different speech sounds there correspond distinct patterns of lip movement and mouth shaping. Part of what enables us to succeed in hearing the speech sounds correctly is that we see what sounds are being produced. It's important to realize that it is difficult to hear speech sounds. The acoustic stimulus is liable to be heard in different ways. We experience this when we try to spell an unfamiliar word or an unusual name on the telephone. If you want to be sure that the airline people get your name right, you had better spell it out using conventional ways of naming the letters (e.g., "Romeo" for r, "Alpha" for a, etc.). Otherwise, they just won't be able to understand you.

A demonstration of the robustness of the influence of seeing on hearing is the McGurk effect, named after the developmental psychologist Harry McGurk. You hear a recording of someone saying "ba," but you see a synchronized video image of someone saying "ga." What you experience is the video head producing the sound "da." Whatever the details of the explanation of this phenomenon, the basic idea would seem to be clear: we use information in the acoustic stimulus and information in what we see—how the mouth is moving—in order to achieve a perception of a speech sound itself. If these sources of information are not consistent with each other, our ability to perceive correctly what is said breaks down.

It is probable that our ability to hear words also depends, to some degree, on our knowledge of what is being talked about and our expectations of what will come next. The linguist Geoffrey Pullum once offered a nice example of this in conversation. You say to someone: "Here is a hat, here is a scarf, here is a dlove." Invariably he or she will hear that last word "glove." "Hat" and "scarf" prime the listener for another article of winter clothing, such as a glove; moreover, the "dl" sound just doesn't occur in English.

Returning to the rubber-hand illusion: we might have thought that when it comes to feeling being touched, or feeling touched on your right hand, there's no need for disambiguation—that is, no need for contextual clues about where and how you are being touched. After all, don't feelings exhibit their intrinsic quality in their very occurrence? But in fact there is need for interpretation or comprehension. You may be touched on your hand, but you will feel yourself touched on the place where you seem to see yourself being touched. Now, in one sense this is clearly an illusion. After all, you really are being touched on your right hand under the table. But in another sense there's no illusion—or rather, the mechanisms at work in this illusion, if we want to call it that, are those of normal, successful perception. Granted, the rubber hand isn't a part of you. But what explains this is not the mere fact that it is a rubber hand, or that it is not connected to your body. The more fundamental fact is that you and the rubber hand have distinct fates. There is nothing more than a superficial and accidental coordination of your experience with the rubber hand. Your own hand, by contrast, is reliably implicated in your sensory and motor interactions with the world around you and with your other sensory experiences. If it were possible to incorporate the rubber hand into a dynamic of active engagement with the world and the body, then, to that degree, the rubber hand would become a part of you.

We have a very special relationship with our own bodies. Evolution itself is to thank for this, no doubt. But the rubber-hand demonstration causes us to rethink what the special relationship is. It does not consist merely of the fact that my hands and arms, say, channel nerve tissue into me, or rather, into my brain. Connectedness, attachment, contiguity—these are important, but mere connectedness or attachment yields only a superficial explanation of what the body is. What makes connection and contiguity important is that they themselves track coordination and common fate. This is the hand—my hand—whose movements I see when I look. Part of what makes it my hand is that I see it grasping the cup. Part of what makes it my hand is the fact that it is the one with which I grasp the cup. Indeed, there is no specific feeling or characteristic sensation that is or would be the feeling that this is my hand. I feel with it (e.g., the cup is too hot!) and in it (I am being tapped and stroked!).

Its "mine"-ness consists in the way it is actively, dynamically, visually involved in my living.

Maurice Merleau-Ponty, the French philosopher, has made just these points. Our lives take place in a setting. This setting—the floor, the walls, the noise, the outside—is the background for whatever activity we are engaged with, such as driving, or walking, or baking a cake. The body, for Merleau-Ponty, shows up as mine (or yours) in just this way as the background condition of my carrying on as I do. These hands belong to me, for it is with them that I break the eggs and mix the batter. As Merleau-Ponty puts it: "The body is the vehicle of being in the world, and having a body is, for a living creature, to be intervolved in a definite environment, to identify oneself with certain projects and be continually committed to them."

## PHANTOM HANDS

The rubber-hand phenomenon shows that I can have sensation in an object that is not, in fact, attached to me. I have suggested this is because attachment or connectedness is not necessary for something to be a part of me. Further support for this idea is found in the phenomenon of the phantom limb, a topic discussed in the last chapter. We now know that when a hand is lost to amputation or accident, one does not automatically lose feeling or sensation in what is now an absent and thus phantom hand. This makes perfect sense if, as I am arguing, what makes a hand yours is its involvement with your habits and projects. I still imagine that I hear the rattle of my dog's collar in the night, even though he has been dead more than a year, and I still automatically grope for the light switch on the wall when I enter the room even though I know perfectly well that the switch has been moved. Just as moving the light switch doesn't stop you from reaching, so the loss of a hand does not all at once obliterate the behavioral setting on which your having or believing yourself to have a hand depends. Just as you don't fully feel the absence of your deceased loved one until the time comes when you go to the phone to call him, as Merleau-Ponty once noticed, so the absence of your hand is not real until it fails to be at your disposal when you prepare to reach with it or stop your fall with it. A limb is quasipresent as a phantom limb when the behavioral, environment-involving attitudes and engagements outlive the loss of the limb. Only when you fully adapt to your new circumstances—only when you break the habit of acting with and on your hand—will your ghost hand finally be put to rest.

The psychologist Vilayanur S. Ramachandran has nicely demonstrated this relationship between the sense of ownership of a part of your body and habits and expectations. Patients with phantom limbs frequently suffer; for example, they complain of cramps in the phantom that they can get no relief from because they can't, as you could with an actual hand, work the cramp out by moving. Ramachandran rigged up a mirror box so that a patient's intact right arm would look, to the patient, like the phantom left arm. Now, in the mirror box, it is possible to turn and move and find soothing relief in the phantom. To paraphrase Botvinick and Cohen, in this therapy the phantom hand feels the relief that the eyes see.

Consciousness does not occur in our brains, and the body is not an elaborate vat for an otherwise autonomous brain. To paraphrase Merleau-Ponty, our body is ours—the place where we feel and the means by which we act—insofar as the current of activity that flows toward the world passes through it.

## THE BODY SCHEMA

Psychologists use the term "body schema" to refer to the implicit, practical body plan that enables us to deploy our bodies effectively in movement and action. You don't need to locate your hands before you put them to use in reaching for something, and as a general rule you don't need to pay attention to your body parts (hands, fingers, whatever) in order to use them effectively. In fact, unless you are very much a novice—an absolute beginner learning a musical instrument, for example—you will disrupt your performance if you focus not on the task at hand, or the goal, but on the bodily mechanics of execution. It isn't that the body is not present to us, or that the body is utterly transparent in our dealings with things around us. We do have a sense of our bodies as present. But in the course of engaged activity, the body doesn't make itself felt as an object of contemplation or awareness. Consider: getting through a doorway never presents itself to you as a problem in the way that, say, getting a couch through the doorway does—and not just because doors are designed to be easy for us to pass through. The point is that we don't need to think about our bodies or pay attention to them to act. We do need to think about the couch to carry it from here to there. The body is present in our normal, active, engaged experience in a different way, comparable to the way in which the periphery of the visual field is present as part of the background against which you attend or focus on this or that. We can be more precise still: the body is present schematically as a range of possibilities of movement or action. That's what the body schema is. For example, my arms can be present to me now, even though I am not now thinking of them; the feeling of their presence comes down to such things as my sense that the coffee cup on the table is within reach. To have a normal, well-functioning body schema, then, is for one to have habits of bodily activity; it is for one to have a body ready in the background to serve one's engaged activities. This unarticulated and perhaps inarticulable knowledge of the body's readiness and availability with its natural degrees of freedom of movement supplies the foundation of everything we do.

The body schema can be contrasted with the body image. The body image is a kind of mental picture that we have of our selves. The anorexic teenager who looks at her emaciated frame in the mirror and feels fat has, in this sense of the term, a damaged body image. Her body schema is likely to be just fine. Her hands and limbs and eyes and head get mobilized in action in the normal way; they are present to her in the background in the normal way. Her problem is that she feels bad about her body, about how it looks and about her ability to control it.

The rubber-hand experiment and the phenomenon of the phantom limb demonstrate that our body schemas can be shaped or altered. Merely losing a limb in an accident doesn't alter the body schema; that's why the phantom lives on. And merely being a detached bit of plastic or rubber is not enough to prevent something from getting incorporated into the body schema.

## EXTENDING THE BODY

One of the simplest ways we extend beyond the limits of our brains and bodies is by using tools. Take the case of a blind person who uses a cane to perceive the ground before him. He feels the texture of the ground at the end of the cane. He feels in the cane even though there are no nerve endings in the cane, even though the cane is a bit of metal or wood. What this shows is not that cane-aided perception is independent of the brain and nervous system; hardly. The point, rather, is that cane-aided perception is not a matter of having feelings either in the end of the cane or in one's hand. The brain and nervous system, insofar as they enable perceptual awareness of the environment, are not in the business of generating feeling; rather, they are in the business of enabling us to interact dynamically with the environment. Our experience and capacities depend on the full character of that skillful interaction. Where we are depends, in significant part, on what we're doing. And what we are—Is the cane a part of me or not? What are the limits of my body? Of myself?—depends on more than the brain alone. Skillful experience with a cane can actually extend the body beyond its strictly biological limits.

These examples show that tool use can modify our body schema. By integrating the tool into a practical repertoire, we are able to remap our expectations of what we can do and so, in effect, we remap the body schema. Drivers can come to feel where the back of the car is as they back into a parking spot, and they can come to sense their contact with the texture of the road through their wheels. In this same way, the baseball glove or lacrosse stick extends the athlete's reach.

As our body schema changes, our relation to the world around us changes, and so how we perceive the environment changes. How big a parking spot looks will be affected by the size of the vehicle you're driving; how steep a hill looks has been shown to vary, depending on the weight of the pack you are carrying. Indeed, it has been shown that the apparent size of the baseball varies in direct correspondence to the hitter's batting average. The better you are hitting, the bigger the speeding balls you are trying to hit will seem! When you're slumping, the balls actually appear to shrink!

These changes in our body schema correspond to processes of neural adaptation. It has been shown, famously, that monkeys using a rake, for example, exhibit enlarged cortical representations of the hand and arm. That is, cells that are sensitive to both the look and the feel of the hand and arm come to treat the rake extension of the arm as if it were part of the body—as if it were the arm.

When our body schema is in this way transformed, our sense of what is near us also changes. We can map space independently of ourselves, but we can also map it in relation to ourselves. Some regions of space are near us or within reach. Psychologists call this peripersonal space. Other regions are beyond reach. This is extrapersonal space. Transformations of the body schema can bring about extensions of peripersonal into what was merely extrapersonal space. Remarkably, human neuropsychology patients who exhibit symptoms of disordered body schema in nearby peripersonal space, but not in more distant extrapersonal space, will begin to show symptoms in extrapersonal space if their dealings with that space depend on skillful tool use. The acquisition of tool-using skills has the effect of increasing the extent of peripersonal space. What was far becomes near.

What are the limits of the plasticity of the body schema? Some degree of plasticity is obviously necessary. After all, through childhood and indeed to a lesser degree roughout lives, we grow, our bodies change, our degrees of freedom alter. Imagine if one were unable to accommodate the shifting sands of one's bodily geometry and changing abilities. Such a deficit would be devastating. One's body would be like an unfamiliar apparatus: learning to be in one's own skin would be like learning to ride a bike or learning to dance the salsa.

Where do we stop, and where does the rest of the world begin? What these reflections on the body schema show is that there's no principled reason even to think that our bodies stop where we think they do. Parts of me—tools—can be spatially discontinuous with me: What makes them me, what makes them part of my body, is the way my actions take them up. And insofar as I act in and feel with my extended body, my mind is extended too.

None of this is meant to challenge the pivotal role of the brain and nervous system in the whole story. But we can acknowledge this fact without conceding that the brain and nervous system are the whole story. For it is only the brain and nervous system in action that allows for a body schema, and we can understand the coming to be of this distributed self only by focusing our attention on the animal or person in action, acting on and acted on by the environment.

## KNOWING ONE'S WAY ABOUT

Do you know what time it is? If you're like most people, you'll say yes and then you'll look at your watch. You believe that you know the time now because you know that you can look at your watch. As the philosopher Andy Clark has convincingly argued, we find it natural to think that we know the time even when, in fact, we don't have as it were the actual time in our heads. We know the time when we have quick, easy, reliable access to that information. The actual repository of information about the time—the watch—is on your wrist, not in your head. In this example, the watch functions as a bit of exterior machinery for supporting your cognitive accomplishment of knowing the time.

Most of us can get around in big cities with tolerable ease and without undue exertion. We know how to get from here to there not because we have actually memorized the map of the whole city; most of us, even in cities where we have lived our whole lives, rely on all manner of external markers, signs, landmarks, and maps to find our ways about. My hometown is New York City. If I come up out of the subway in an unfamiliar part of town, I can usually figure out how I stand in relation to things around me. The sign says "Second Avenue." I know that traffic on Second Avenue runs downtown, so I know that traffic is heading south. It's easy enough, then, to tum about and head off to the West Side. Navigation requires that we use our senses, that we pay attention to landmarks, and that we draw on background knowledge too (e.g., that Second Avenue runs downtown).

Now, my ability to find my way around New York City is a cognitive ability, an intellectual achievement, albeit a humble one. But it is one that I possess only given my situation—that is, given the larger context of my access to environmental markers and cues. The environment itself is what enables me to find my way around in it. My understanding, my knowledge, is not something autonomous, something detachable. Rather, it is a skillful familiarity with and integration into the world. Just as we may count on our fingers and calculate with pen and paper, so we navigate with the world. Like my brain, my body, my eyes, and the city itself belong to what enables me to find my way about.

I agree with the philosophers Andy Clark and David Chalmers that there is no principled reason not to think of the wristwatch, the landmarks, the pen and paper, the linguistic community, as belonging to my mind. The causal processes that enable us to talk and think and find our ways around are not confined to what is going on in our skulls. But that is just a way of saying that the machinery of the mind itself is not confined to the skull. The head is not a magical membrane. We are involved with the world around us. We are in it and of it.

## REAL PRESENCE

We ourselves are distributed, dynamically spread-out, world-involving beings. We are not world representers. We have no need for that idea. To put the point in a provocative way, we are, in Merleau-Ponty's memorable phrase, "empty heads turned toward the world." And as a result of this, our worlds are not confined to what is inside us, memorized, represented. Much more is present to us than is immediately present. We live in extended worlds where much is present virtually, thanks to our skills and to technology. Consider a simple example but one of enormous richness. You experience the house as having a back, even though you can't see the back from where you are. You do not merely think or judge that there is a back. Nor do you merely infer that there is a back. The back feels present. In my view the back of the house is present to my visual experience of the house, even though it is hidden, because its being hidden does not prevent me from having bodily access to it. Movement of my body in relation to the house—walking around it—will bring it into view; my experience right now of the house has that contour. It is structured by the fact that now, in front of the house, I am related to the back of the house by possible movements. The back of the house is present as absent—that is to say, as out of view.

We can think of this as a kind of virtual presence, but only if we recognize that all presence is virtual in this way—not in the sense of being false, or illusory, or less than genuine, but in the sense that the world is present as reachable, rather than as depicted. And in that sense our relation to the back of the house is not different from our relation to the house's front. We bear a relation to the house: the house itself, the back no less than the front (or the front, no less than the back), is within reach.

Technology increases the scope of our access, and so it increases the extent of what is or can be present for us. My mother thousands of miles away is present, for she is just a phone call away.

The funds in my U.S. bank account are available to me here in Germany in this age of electronic banking, and so they are, in that sense, present—that is to say, they feel present to me.

The use of instant messaging provides a striking example of this kind of extended presence. Studies have shown that the use of messaging among teenagers in Japan has transformed the dynamics of social relations. Kids text back and forth throughout the day. They rarely send informative or detailed messages; the informational content of their sendings tends to be minimal. In effect, they are "pinging" each other: letting each other know that they are online, or in reach, or "there." Before school, during school, on the bus home after school: ping ping ping— the reassuring indication that your friend is there for you. In this way, the practice of texting, or instant messaging, creates a new modality of social presence. Just as tools can warp the body schema and connect me to bits of stuff by making that stuff in effect part of me, so the pinging action of instant messaging can enable individuals separated by space across Tokyo to operate socially within each other's sphere. They are virtually present to each other.

A case can be made that joint presence in an actual shared physical space is the best kind of presence. We are embodied biological creatures and evolution has conditioned us perfectly to fit into actual physical niches. We are naturally attuned to the physical environment and to each other. Physical contact is polymodal: we hear the words and see the facial expressions and feel the heat of each other's breath and jointly attend to what is going on around us. Virtual worlds, in comparison, are thin in a distinctively digital way. I don't mean that virtual presence is merely illusory. It is real presence extended by new and different methods. There is something vaguely disturbing about the thought that passively sitting at a computer, reading and typing, could be a genuinely active, outgoing, socially engaged mode of being. But that is exactly what it is.

EDITOR'S NOTE

Have neurobiology and communication technology changed what we might have been familiar with as modular orientation systems—to structure the dimensions of time and space, for instance? This is one of the key topics discussed by Alva Noë in his book *Out of Our Heads: Why You Are Not Your Brain, and Other Lessons from the Biology of Consciousness* (2009), from which pages 67–84 have been reprinted here. Instead of consciousness originating in our brain, feelings or sensations emerge from what we do and how we interact with the environment. Noë's question 'Where do you stop and where does the rest of the world begin?' goes right to the core of contemporary discussion on modularity. If we think of singular units as dynamic parts, the challenge for modular systems today is to define connections rather than hard-edged borders.

AUTHOR'S NOTES

The epigraph for this chapter is taken from Dewey's essay "The new psychology." This was published in the *Andover Review* 2 (1884): 278—289. I made use of a copy of the text available online at the York University Classics in the history of Psychology website, at psych-classics.yorku.ca/.

The rubber-hand illusion was first reported by M. Botvinick and J. Cohen in *Nature* 391, no. 6669: 756. It has also been investigated by V. S. Ramachandran. His work on this topic, as well as on the topic of phantom limbs, is discussed in his book (cowritten with Sandra Blakeslee) *Phantoms in the Brain* (New York: William Morrow, 1998).

The McGurk Effect was first reported in 1978 by Harry McGurk and John MacDonald in 'Hearing lips and seeing voices,' in *Nature* 264: 746–748. Dominic Massaro at the University of California, Santa Cruz, has argued persuasively that *vision* plays a crucial role in normal speech perception. He puts this finding to use in his work with deaf children.

My own study of the problem of phantom limbs was carried out jointly with Susan Hurley. [...] Merleau-Ponty's ideas about phantom limbs and the body schema are to be found in his *Phenomenology of Perception,* especially in the chapter called 'The body as object and mechanistic physiology.' I quote in the text from page 82 of the translation by Colin Smith (London: Routledge and Kegan Paul, 1962). For an excellent development of Merleau-Ponty's ideas, and an introduction to him, see writing by Shaun Gallagher, especially his book *How the Body Shapes the Mind* (Oxford: Oxford University Press, 2005). The neuroscientist Marcel Kinsbourne has incorporated some of these ideas in his writing. I recommend, in particular, his 'Awareness of one's own body: an attention theory of its nature, development and basis,' in *The Body and The Self,* edited by J. L. Bermudez, A. Marcel, and N. Eilan (Cambridge, MA: MIT Press, 1995, pages 225–245).

Gareth Evans observed that we do not need to think about how to get ourselves through doors in the way that we need to think about how to get a couch through a door. The latter, but not the former, is a problem for spatial cognition. See his *Varieties of Reference* (Oxford: Oxford University Press, 1982).

Dennis R. Proffitt and his University of Virginia PhD student Jessica K. Witt have shown that the perceived size of a baseball correlates with batting average. See their paper 'See the ball, hit the ball' in the December 2005 issue of *Psychological Science*. They have also shown that inclined paths look steeper to tired hikers: see 'Perceived slant: a dissociation between perception and action,' in *Perception* 36, no. 2 (2007): 249–57. Yoshiaki Iwamura, Atsushi ltiki, and Michio Tanaka, in a 1996 paper in *Neuroreport*, showed that tool use can modify the body schema. For a general review of this area of research, see Nicholas Holmes and Charles Spence's 'The body schema and the multisensory representation(s) of peripersonal space,' in *Cognitive Process* 5, no. 2 (June 2004): 94–105.

Andy Clark and David J. Chalmers's essay 'The extended mind,' in *Analysis* 58, no. 1 (1998): 7–19, presents an argument that we should consider artifacts outside the head to belong to the "machinery of cognition" (to use Rick Grush's phrase). Anyone who appreciates that sometimes we think with words, or with our pens, or with our paintbrushes, can appreciate this insight. Clark has just published a new book on this "extended mind" hypothesis; it includes a foreword by Chalmers: see *Supersizing the Mind: Embodiment, Action, and Cognitive Extension* (New York: Oxford University Press, 2008). Notably, neither Clark nor Chalmers has sympathy for the idea developed here that consciousness itself can be explained only if we make use of such an extended conception of the machinery of mind. Conscious experience would seem to be detachable from and independent of the world without. I return to this topic in Chapter 8 [of *Out of Our Heads*].

There's a lot of literature about new media and the ways they are changing our relations with others and our sense of ourselves. My comments in the text about instant messaging and Japanese teenagers draw on the research of Peter Lyman and Mimi Ito. I am grateful, in particular, to Peter Lyman (now deceased) for his helpful guidance.

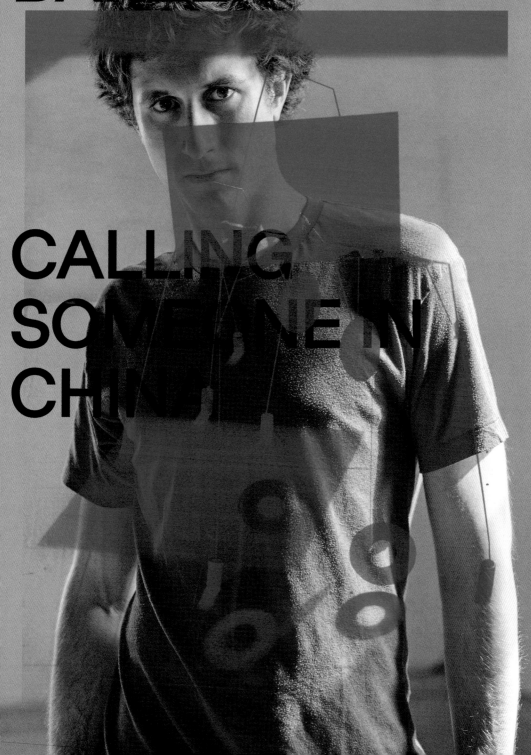

DIMITRI
BÄHLER

CALLING
SOMEONE IN
CHINA

# Calling Someone in China

## Interview with Dimitri Bähler

I

INTERVIEWER   You seem to have an interest in different types of production: industrial production, crafts that might be disappearing, and potential collaborations with customers who decide how they want their lamp to look within the modular system of a product's design. How do you combine these different modes in your work?

DIMITRI BÄHLER   Yes, I am interested in different types of production. The difference for me is mainly the context of the project. In Burkina Faso, for example, craftsmanship is much more common than in Switzerland, giving rise to possibilities that perhaps don't exist in Western Europe. On the other hand, if you have to design something that needs to be produced easily, it needs different working principles that relate to the facilities available to a manufacturer.

Surprisingly, sometimes, a 'hand-made' project that you'd never consider being produced on a larger scale could actually be manufactured with a few modifications. This is true of some of the products we are working on with Moustache, a French furniture design company based in Paris.

↑ Dimitri Bähler's masterclass at work, 2014

→ → Presentation by Dimitri Bähler's masterclass at the Domaine de Boisbuchet, France, 2014

When I start a new project, my approach is always very hands-on. The closest I've come to industrial production so far has been working on projects for HAY, a Danish furnishing and accessories company, such as 'UU' (a wooden pencil holder, designed in collaboration with Linn Kandel and Ismaël Studer) and the 'Volet' hooks, made of anodized folded aluminium. For these projects, it was essential to build models and prototypes, and to speak with those who work in the manufacturing process in order to achieve the highest-quality result.

In the end, these different methods of production exert a mutual influence on each other. I really like to work in a flexible and intuitive way. It makes it more difficult to be placed in category— so perhaps I'm less relevant commercially, but I'm open and well connected to different production contexts instead.

I understand your work as very visual and playful. Is there a connection between your designs—the 'La Coutard' lamp, for example—and modularity?

DB    I would say yes—most of the time. Often what I design is like a system that I can apply to a series of objects. Some of my projects are more modular at the level of production, as with the length and the height of 'UU', for example, but some of them are modular at a user level, such as 'La Coutard'. That was a design I produced in 2008–09 et ECAL, and it was inspired by a 1988 documentary by Alain Cavalier called *24 Portraits*, which looked at crafts that might disappear in the 21st century in Western Europe. The lamp is based on twenty triangular elements that are industrially produced, and that are modular in the way they are assembled because of the flexibility of their connections. I created a contrast in the production methods by industrially fabricating the triangles and then having the lamp finished in traditional caning. The interest lies in those two different processes. I think modularity plays a visual role, since objects must be combined in order to work, and it also creates rules, a framework—a kind of grammar you can work with. Simple modules are like letters, arranged in such as a way to form words, sentences and books. Ultimately, it enables communication. That's what I aimed for with 'La Coutard': I wanted to enable communication between the different people involved in the project: me as the designer, manufacturers, sellers and users.

Do you think that modular systems in general or objects that are made of modular parts can ever achieve a final, finished state?

DB    No. The essence of a modular system is that it is never finished. It is an ever-growing, ever-changing system. That is what modularity is all about. It is exactly those qualities that we wanted to work on in our installation. The movement, the interaction, the communication between the different modules never stops. On the other hand, the module itself, the brick, has to be designed in a final state, like a piece of Lego. It has to have a precise goal, a function, which is to build a bigger ensemble. Now imagine if the modules themselves had a precise function but were malleable—like brain neurons, for instance, which constantly adapt, building new circuits for storing and processing information. Their make-up is flexible. Computers and new materials

→ Dimitri Bähler,
'La Coutard', 2009

↓ Dimitri Bähler,
moulds for 'Patterns
& Colours', 2013

→→ Dimitri Bähler's
masterclass at work,
2014

or components are moving in that direction, with ever-more complex coding or forms of intelligence that look more and more like that of a human brain. Computers are of course based on a modular system. They assemble the same two components—the figures 0 and 1—in a precise sequence in order to form information. Possibilities grow exponentially with the amount of modular parameters you use. It is like a probability formula. The challenge is then to choose the best solution.

I found it very interesting that, from the very beginning of your USM masterclass, you linked the subject of modularity to interaction. Together with the participants, you created a moving installation made up of four modules that react to computational coding but also to natural forces such as gravity. What are the modular features of this kind of interaction, and how do the modules interact?

DB   Modularity means that you can adapt, assemble or play with the different modules to build your own system. Interaction is the action of adapting and playing. That is why I made this shortcut: modularity is interaction. As for our project, I wanted to work on something that shows this active process in a more visual and poetic way, illustrating how the creator or user interacts with the system, and how objects and systems can communicate with each other. Our project deals with the laws of nature, such as gravity and pressure. That makes the programmed output more random and adaptive—more like a living being.

So you say that modularity is interaction, and you also talk about modularity being a form of communication. When you look at your masterclass project, where do you see the difference between interaction and communication?

DB   For me, the idea of communication is that there is a purpose behind it. It is an exchange of information, a message that you send and interpret. I would say the main difference between the two is that, in communication, there is a more visual or audible nuance. Interaction can be silent: it is more about a change of state combined with the idea of movement, but without a definite, necessary purpose.

Presentation by Dimitri Bähler's masterclass
at the Domaine de Boisbuchet, France, 2014

But both terms are alike in that they convey a sense
of energy travelling between one component and the
next. For a product designer, this project is interesting
because it brings up very specific technical as well
as aesthetic questions. Allan Wexler said that it's like
calling someone in China: the phone is a physical
representation of an invisible connection. This
installation can likewise be understood as an abstract
way of showing the process of communication: it
resembles a deconstructed, visible computer, defined

by physical movement as well as electronics. The characteristic of this project is that the system follows a programmed random code as well as the laws of nature. The system is responsive: when you tickle it, it wakes up and moves. The different installations are electronically connected, but always in a different order. The initial impulse is given by a person blowing onto a little windmill, but the energy is spread throughout the whole system like air into the lungs of a living being. A breath is amplified and makes the different surfaces move in space, creating in a choreography of shapes.

II
Dimitri, the interactive installation you're showing at the exhibition in Milan is astonishingly close to the initial concept you developed during the masterclass, and it's clearly a much smoother version of that idea. One thing that's different now, if I've understood correctly, is that instead of having, as it were, a chain of communication in which the initial impulse is given at the beginning and then moves from machine to machine to machine, now the machines seem to react to each other in new, more complex ways.

DB    It is a smoother idea of our initial concept, but on a larger scale, and that was a challenge. The exhibition space in Milan has influenced the dimensions of the installation a lot …

Basically, the parameters presented by the space and the materials were the main issues that arose during the project development. They encouraged a lot of productive and interesting discussions between designers concerning the module's different movements. It took quite a long time for the whole group to define every detail and its effect on the timeline of movements as well as its choreography in the exhibition space—but it was definitely a very interesting process to follow.

The programming was different as well. Before, during the masterclass at the Domaine de Boisbuchet, there was just a chain reaction that always followed the same order, but now we've decided to give the whole installation a kind of standby mode, so that when there are no users the installation breezes away gently, but as soon as you trigger it you start one of the four modules always in a random order.

What was the thinking behind this new element of randomness?

DB   I think it better matches the concept that we had at the beginning at the masterclass: the idea that modularity is perceived as something more closely related to human beings. The idea was to make a link between the machine and the person. So if, for instance, you blow gently onto the windmill here, you will just start one installation—one machine, let's say—but if you blow more, it will start the whole installation working, and always in a random pattern.[1] It's more flexible, in the way that neurons build new connections in the brain to respond to a new necessity.

↑→ 'Networks in Motion', project designed by Dimitri Bähler's masterclass, exhibition view, Milan, 2015

Dimitri Bähler, one of the tutors of seven USM masterclasses, was interviewed during the 'rethink the modular' workshop at the Domaine de Boisbuchet, France, 2014 (I), and on the occasion of the 'rethink the modular' exhibition in Milan, 2015 (II).

1   To see a video of the installation at work, please visit https://vimeo.com/124519772 [last accessed 11 November 2015].

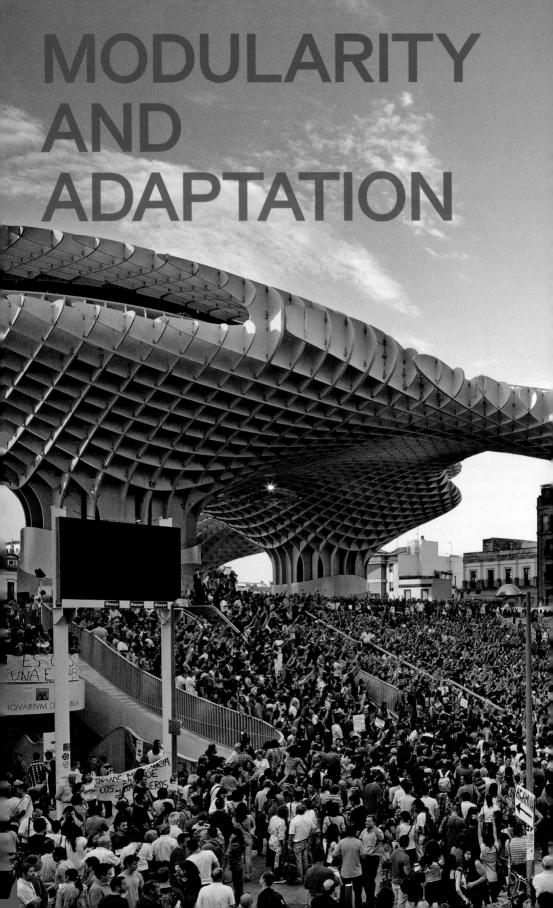

# MODULARITY
# AND
# ADAPTATION

THOMAS
DIENES

JÜRGEN
MAYER H.

# Modularity and Adaptation

## Thomas Dienes
## Jürgen Mayer H.

THOMAS DIENES   When I began studying architecture, it was extremely important to implement both industrial production methods and industry-related design principles in the planning and construction processes. But if I take a look around at contemporary architecture, not many of these ideas have been developed further. From my point of view, thinking about modular systems in architecture still offers great potential—but we might have to consider different parameters from those of forty or fifty years ago. I am very interested to hear more about your experiences in dealing with standardization on one hand, and solutions that might be adapted to future changes on the other. Are there modular systems that can bridge those two demands in your current work as an architect?

JÜRGEN MAYER H.   My answer goes in two directions. You have modularity in prefabrication for quite specific elements in architecture, where a certain geometric complexity and quality of detail cannot be realized any more on the construction site. Instead, you use certain tools to prefabricate, translating this complexity to the construction site. Of course, there's also a cost issue in terms of mass production. The questions are how prefabricated elements will change the way we think of architectural production and how they affect building costs in general. I was in India recently, where prefab companies basically produce everything from structural elements to elements needed for fitting out, automatically and at the right time. The process is also inexpensive and very successful commercially. I suppose that works better for architecture in a large open space, but when it comes to buildings in an urban setting, the limits become more rigid, and prefabrication might not be as successful. There's always a little buffer zone where you have to mediate between the system and the context, and maybe that's the interesting part of architecture. There are cost issues and issues surrounding modularity, in addition to a certain complexity that can no longer be reproduced at the construction site; but in architecture there's also the matter of sustainability, which reduces construction time. When you prefabricate, you reduce the noise and dust pollution on site. So it has also other effects, and it might actually result in better-quality detailing and materials. It's interesting for the way we think about architecture, but it's not really part of the current production process or the building industry. I don't know yet how much we would give up and how much we would gain through this transformation. Prefabricated modular systems in the building industry affect the way we think in terms of design, because they are based on certain grids that might become a new standard.

TD    There are also shifts in modular thinking as far as furniture is concerned. At USM we are receiving more and more special requests by end users for modifications, for instance. A modular system like USM Haller offers a limited number of individual parts, produced industrially to a very high quality standard. But the user can employ them to build an individual world—a little like the principle behind Lego. Of course, it will be a world circumscribed by the system's rules. You could compare it to the example you've given, of the difference between an architectural development on an open site and one in an old city or a space where a lot of other parameters already exist.

JMH    Taking that a little further, several different ways of considering modularity are coming to mind. Take our Metropol Parasol in Seville, for example, and the way it is constructed. It is like an organic shape that had to be broken down into smaller elements or modules for prefabrication. You can see this design and production process in the final product. In that sense, it is very accessible and transparent when it comes to understanding the structure and the site. At the same time—owing to digitalization in both design and fabrication—prefabrication allowed for a certain flexibility of shape adapted specifically to this urban context. We considered how different user groups would spend their time in different zones of the Metropol Parasol: the space could be used for

J. Mayer H. Architects, 'Metropol
Parasol', Seville, 2011

religious processions, sporting events, corporate presentations or political demonstrations. We also have parts that can actually function like local neighbourhoods, such as the small bars under the parasol. It allows for a great deal of flexibility within one structure and seems to work really well. Coming back to the USM Haller system—how do you deal with customers' needs for more flexibility or specific modifications? Have there been attempts to introduce flexibility of shape into the system? The modular idea seems to be very strong, and I do not know of any 'breakouts' or special add-ons, apart from colour choices and perhaps the materials' surface finish.

TD   Yes, there has been the idea of modifying the USM Haller system, and USM has increased the number of parts over time. But it has always been a controversial discussion within the company. If you are operating within a system with a limited set of parts, every time you offer a broader range of available parts, the level of flexibility is simultaneously decreased. The more parts you offer, the less flexible your system is at the end. Again, Lego is a good example here. When I was a child, I had a big box of bricks but only a few different components, which I used to build my imaginary worlds. Now when I choose a present for a child, what I see at the toy store is the aeroplane, car or ship itself. If I hand this set of very specialized Lego to the child, what will result is most likely an aeroplane, a car or a ship—instead of an endless world of imaginable shapes.

JMH   People usually buy USM Haller because they like it and they want it as it is. It has already become a classic; it's already a finished product to a certain extent. To create something out of it might be a challenging task. I don't know if it actually needs to happen within the USM Haller system or whether you would need to develop something completely new.

TD   We have to proceed with developing the classic USM Haller system, but very carefully. Some additional functions might be integrated, but these would be almost invisible features, such as soft-close mechanisms. Besides keeping the USM Haller system up to date, USM is also planning totally new furniture elements. In order to relate to existing products, they have to be connected to them in some way, by means of a shared grid or other modular principle. The vertical elements of the 'Privacy Panels'—a product that was launched in 2015—can be attached to the classic Haller tables, for instance, or they can also be used as free-standing walls in an open space. The 'panel family' now constitutes a kit of ten different elements. Panels can be arranged in various ways according to changing needs, dividing interior spaces or absorbing noise—an effect that can be adapted to invididual needs without rebuilding the existing structure.

JMH  It's one thing to define a standard element and another to connect it to another system. When you look at the façade we built for an apartment block on the Johannesstrasse, Berlin, it had a specific profile owing to the way the wall elements protruded from the overall support, but each element was treated differently and had its own curves. Standardization and specification went hand in hand, and I think that's where intelligence was required, allowing these two to come together and create something specific and new.

TD  With a new product, it's not so much about reproducing a similar design to the USM Modular Furniture Haller system. That wouldn't work. But by linking a new product to shared modular principles, such as a similar grid, it becomes connectable. Something unexpected happened when we introduced a new material. It took around five years to develop the 'Privacy Panels' in collaboration with the design studio Atelier Oï. They suggested working with a very soft textile. The idea was that you could combine an industrial building material such as metal with the softer feel of clothing and pillows. The result was a very light structure that is related also to people's clothing as well as to furniture or architecture. So maybe this new panel structure will change the overall effect of USM Haller if the two systems meet. From the point of view of materials and design, we are very open to the future. At the same time we will preserve the main principles of modularity and system thinking from the Haller system.

JMH  Are there new requirements or new interests that might have an effect on what is already in production? Why do you feel you need to update the system or to develop new systems for the future?

TD  Keeping USM Haller up to date means paying attention to the details. For example, people are using soft-close mechanisms in their kitchens and are now asking for the same functions in USM Haller furniture. If you store china in a cabinet and move to shut the door, for the last 5 or 6 centimetres (2 inches) the door closes smoothly and automatically clicks shut very softly. This is one of these projects where we have to develop something new but from the engineering side. Looking at workplaces of the future, ten years ago we thought that offices would be paperless. Of course this didn't happen, but what we noticed was that people were storing less and less close to their workstations. So storage will be different in the future from what it is now. Desks will have new and different functionalities integrated into them—they will be wired in a certain way or be highly adjustable for ergonomic

USM Privacy Panels, 'Make it yours!'
advertising campaign, 2016

reasons. The topic of 'open plan' has raised its head again for the first time in a long while. Trying to introduce a structure into existing spaces that are perhaps very different is one issue. And when you work with open-plan spaces, acoustics are more and more of an issue as well.

JMH    Adaptability and flexibility in architecture are also connected to the commercial success of buildings. You could also argue that it's sustainable if an office building can turn into an apartment building or vice versa. You're always dealing with potential changes from the point of users, which is where I think modularity might play an important role in the future. I remember Luigi Snozzi designed a housing project in, I think, the 1970s or 1980s, where a long element at the front had rooms defined as living rooms and bathrooms, but the sleeping rooms at the back could be connected to one apartment or another. If you were older or were the only person living there, you might need only one or two bedrooms. In that case, you could actually give a bedroom to somebody else, to a neighbour if they needed it. I think one of the biggest problems that we face in ageing societies is that the amount of space occupied by a single person doubles the moment somebody dies or moves out. There seems to be no way to adjust to these changes easily. A couple of very interesting projects in Switzerland have tried to reduce the amount of private space taken up by individuals by adding shared kitchens or other facilities, such as laundry rooms or community rooms, to buildings. These are innovative ideas: you can take modules of ownership and start to rethink the idea of sharing. You allocate spaces for specific purposes for specific periods of time, as in a sharing economy.

TD    One of my architecture teachers at the University of Karlsruhe was Ottokar Uhl. Once he cited an example from Vienna showing that, in fact, people very rarely changed the layout of architectural spaces over time, even where this was possible. It was a residential building complex in which a primary and a secondary structure were divided extremely clearly, and it was designed as a modular system. He told the story of an old woman who changed the walls of her flat, but she was probably one of the few who ever made any alterations. So this kind of modular flexibility was mainly a theoretical idea. There is also a difference of scale between furniture and architecture. Are we prepared to incorporate this kind of modular flexibility into buildings? I imagine that, in the near future, there will be new materials and construction methods that will make such changes much easier for users.

JMH    There's another interesting project by Elemental in Chile: a very low-cost housing project in which a certain flexibility is built

←←↑→ Elemental, Quinta Monroy Housing, Iquique, Chile, 2004

in from the start. There is always an empty space left between one house and its neighbour. At first, people might be able to afford only a small house, or one family might live on the ground floor and another on the first floor. But then, as time goes by, they can expand to fill the space between the houses. They can use it first as a garden, then build another room if they need one, and so on, so that the empty space allows them to adapt. But this kind of flexibility only works for growth. The idea of modularity and changeable spaces in architecture was often introduced in the form of container-like solutions in the 1960s and 1970s. That was a very obvious solution to the problem of combining industrial construction in architecture with flexibility for the users. Look at the add-ons at the Nakagin Capsule Tower in Tokyo, for example. These buildings are fantastic experiments, but ultimately they might not be as flexible as they look. I don't see that many have really been extended or modified over the decades.

TD    I agree. Architects and designers have often tried to introduce modular flexibility to spaces where people live. But when you look at them some years later, the structures actually haven't changed very much. This also happens with USM Haller furniture, despite its modular potential. If it's too time-consuming to adapt, a modular system often turns into a permanent structure, and this applies to buildings, too. In an urban context, buildings are integrated in their surroundings, meaning that you have to adhere to certain regulations. In megacities that grow extremely fast, the question of flexibility is related not just to single houses: it's more a question of how flexible the whole structure is in order to deal with rapid expansion. The need to adapt structures will increase in the near future, on the level of both indoor furnishings and city infrastructure.

JMH    Different scales and modules will play a big role in the future development of cities. Perhaps we should speak more of modules than modularity in this context. We worked on a study for the Audi Urban Future Award a couple of years ago. If cars are modules that exchange something with the system of a city, and if you imagine the implications of automated driving or electrified cars, then you are talking about a whole new infrastructure that needs to be implemented within the city: a new electricity network, of course, but also digitalization and the use of apps and social media. A 'smart' city is in control of the logistics that underpin such modules. We will need to manage and to design those logistics. It might even change the way we think about modularity in general. Most of us already have an online identity, and in that expanded sense we've become modules within an urban setting. We might have four identities simultaneously, which you could view as

J. Mayer H. Architects, JOH 3, residential building, Berlin, 2012

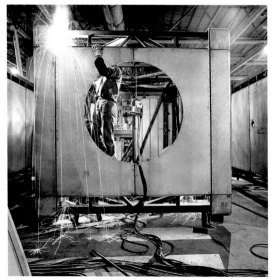

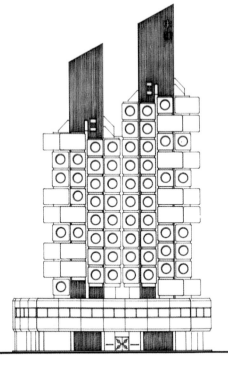

↖ Construction of a capsule for Kisho Kurokawa's Nakagin Capsule Tower, Tokyo

↑ Nakagin Capsule Tower, Tokyo, axonometric drawing

← Nakagin Capsule Tower, Tokyo, 1972

→ Cutaway diagram of a capsule in the Nakagin Capsule Tower, Tokyo

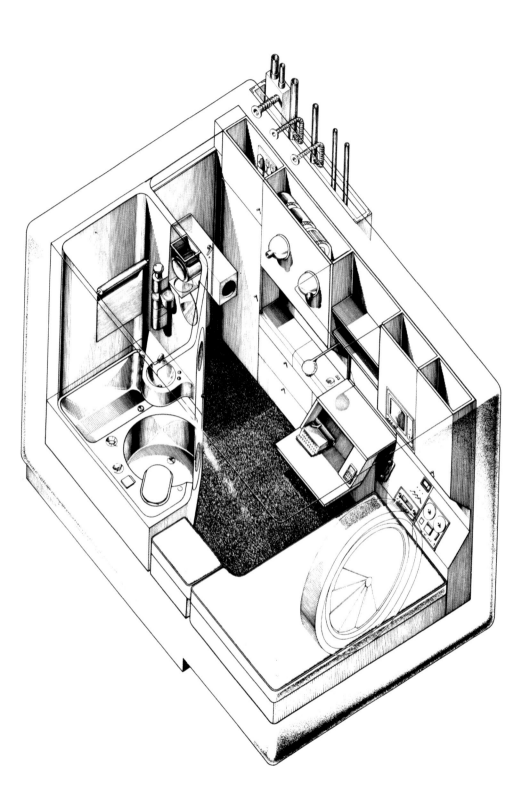

four different modules. Information delivered to you via digital infrastructure leads to alternative ways of navigating through the city and communicating with each other. This is shaping our perception of the environment to a great extent. It's not the idea of the module itself that changes: it's the way we deal and communicate with these modules that leads to a different understanding of the production of space.

TD   It's interesting to think about our changing views on modules. And I assume that the way these modules could be integrated into a system might be more complex in the future. In order for them to work together, to communicate with each other, you need an infrastructure. If you imagine a city in which people are interacting with these new modules, you will also have infrastructure from earlier periods, equipped with very different types of technology. If we think about the question of connecting material to immaterial modules, we also have to think about the small details. We launched some concept furniture in 2012 with the idea of creating a new interface between users and a table. You can adjust the table by spending twenty to thirty seconds pressing buttons, depending on the motor speed needed to raise it from sitting height to standing height or the other way around. The table may look fine, but spending so much time pressing buttons is not ideal. So we decided to develop a better, more intuitive interface between the user's hands and the table. We thought about including voice commands, but there would be a problem with different voices in an open-plan office, since the table would not recognize who was speaking. Using a smartphone app to communicate was also considered, but it was difficult to make a smooth and reliable tool that would work with different operating systems. So we ended up exploring the use of our hands once more, incorporating sensitive parts within the table that would activate a supporting motor. If I press underneath, the top of the table moves up according to the intensity of pressure. This was an interesting prototype, since it involved an attempt to create a truly intuitive interface. I would like to find a kind of intuitive interface for buildings, too—especially when I am travelling. Think of hotels where you can't find the right button to switch off all the lights any more owing to the complex network of electronical interfaces in your room. So how can different types of people, architecture and infrastructure be combined in a city without a loss of communication on an intuitive level?

JMH   Apps and other forms of communication software change the way we share what we own and what we use: we could speak of modules here, too. We lend our car or we borrow something from somebody else, and it represents economic efficiency and ease of use. Some people want to make money with their cars when they're not using them; others don't own a car but rent one when they need it. There's an increasing variety of elements—we have called them modules—out there that have become very personalized and specific. However, although everything is more available than ever before, a certain longing for the special, unique experience becomes an attractive alternative.

TD    I am getting the impression that the more different modules are offered within one system and the more systems I have access to, the more people will try to find a place where they can create a very personal space in their search for the individual and the simple. People are also wanting access to nature once more—away from built or digital modules, so to speak.

JMH    I think the transition from street into building—especially at ground-floor level—is very important in this context. That's where an interior begins—or an interior can become part of the exterior. Today, urban furniture is more than just a bench on which to sit. It may also be a place to escape a busy building, meaning that outdoors might actually be more private than the inside, especially if you work in an open-plan office and are constantly available on different communication channels. Over the past thirty years street life has become better: the air is cleaner in many cities, at least in Europe, and people are spending more and more of the year outside. I think it started with cafes. When I was 18 or 19 years old, there were very few cafes in Stuttgart with outdoor seating. Now outdoors has become an important place to spend time, even during winter thanks to patio heaters. This change occurred from the early 1990s on. There is a kind of 'indoorification' of the outdoors happening at the moment, and the walls between the two are increasingly permeable. It will be interesting to see how questions of privacy change in the future. And if we think of a city as a modular space, there is also a shift from a rather static conception of modular production towards the possibilities of flexible use and a more organic understanding of growth and shrinkage as well. In the end, everything will touch on the potential of connectivity.

This discussion between Thomas Dienes, Head of Group Product Development at USM, and Jürgen Mayer H., an architect specializing in the intersection between architecture, communication and new technology, took place on 15 June 2015 in Berlin.

# LORENZO BINI

# FOR A TREE, MODULARITY IS NOT AN ISSUE

# For a Tree, Modularity is Not an Issue

## Interview with Lorenzo Bini

I    INTERVIEWER   Are modular principles
a fundamental part of any construction?

LORENZO BINI   If I look at architecture as a
finished product, I can see that there are buildings,
whether I like them or not, that do not show their
modularity. On the other hand, if you look at the way
they are built there is always some kind of modular
thinking behind them. If we consider modules as
repeated elements, the most direct and simple
way to think about modularity is to consider the
relationship between different scales and between
human scale and space. Perhaps there are buildings
that totally lack modularity but, if I consider all
the architecture that takes this relationship between
man and space into account, I can hardly think
of anything built without modules or modularity.

What examples come to mind when you think
of architecture that doesn't show modularity?

LB   I can't think of any specific building that hides
the way it's built. I think I could see it in buildings

that feature arbitrary shapes or disorganized spaces, and this is something that works at every scale. It strikes me, for instance, that certain museums feature disorganized signs, fire alarms, switches, emergency lamps and other sorts of elements that are obviously difficult to control. They might just be details, but when we enter a public space or a museum with this characteristic it affects our perception of the space. It's tricky to make these details look unnoticeable, to organize them in such a way that they don't become visually oppressive. I like random things, but in this case it's almost like a lack of attention. There are public spaces where these things are organized, and you immediately notice a more 'domestic' feel. You feel much more at ease when these details are worked out.

> It seems to be important for you to perceive architecture in a certain way, so that if you look at a building you somehow recognize modularity, even if you do so unconsciously.

LB    It doesn't necessarily mean that a building needs to expose the way it's constructed, but maybe there is a relationship between man and space. Making materials visible for what they are is already a way to transfer or express modularity: the way a floor is laid or brick walls are built can refer to the modularity that was embedded in its construction. I wouldn't say it's always good to be able to perceive visually the modules and modularity of a building. Sometimes it

Lorenzo Bini, 'Kosho', temporary structure, 2010

can just work on a psychological level. Architects are obsessed with control. Since we are completely absorbed in building practice—and the design process is just one aspect of that, alongside all the different technical, psychological, social, economic and regulatory considerations—we constantly struggle to keep control of everything that relates to our buildings. At the same time, however, we have to accept a certain degree of tolerance. Even if we must tolerate 'the limits of control' (to quote a movie by Jim Jarmusch), we are always attuned to things that remain hidden to most people. Therefore, architects are constantly—and instinctively—searching for modularity in buildings.

The office building you designed in the Via Zumbini, Milan, resembles an urban structure trying to hide away from the public. Rather than displaying its structure, the building has a fence-like construction around it. Why were you interested in creating this very specific impression, and how did you work with the material?

LB   The project that you refer to, an office building, was originally an industrial building from the 1930s. We were asked to design a very neutral environment, so that whoever moved in could add colours or transform the space. The façade is actually overlooking an inner court—it's not what you see from the street—and this office space does not belong to a single company looking for visibility, but to a variety of tenants. This specific area of Milan is rather suburban and not very hospitable. Actually, the street façades are quite anonymous and very plain, but facing the court is a metal structure. In many ways it's as if we wanted to protect the inside from an aggressive environment through these modules, and the metal does actually look like fencing. But we were actually more concerned with what is between this front layer and the actual façade of the building, because there is a corridor 1.5 metres [5 feet] wide between them. The metal structure also acts as a support for climbing plants that provide shade in summer but die back in the winter.

Is there anyone who has influenced your interest in capturing modularity in architecture?

Lorenzo Bini,
Zumbini office
building, Milan, 2011

LB    Every time I feel like I am in trouble I grab the
Sol LeWitt monograph that is at hand in my office.
Sol LeWitt's work always reminds me of the idea that
complexity is not something you have to pursue for
the sake of complexity. The square or the cube, the
simplest shapes or volumes, can result in high degrees
of complexity. To develop your work you have to
follow a very simple rule in a rigorous manner in
order for it to become the main principle governing

# VARIATIONS OF INCOMPLETE OPEN CUBES

↖ Sol LeWitt, 'Variations of Incomplete
Open Cubes', 1974

← Sigurd Lewerentz, St Peters Church,
Klippan, Sweden, 1966

↑ Isamu Noguchi, playground equipment
for Ala Moana Park, Hawaii, 1940

the whole construction. Sol LeWitt once said that 'irrational thoughts should be followed absolutely and logically'.[1] Another important reference in this regard is Sigurd Lewerentz's church in Klippan. Lewerentz decided that he wanted to build the entire church without cutting a single brick—and he did. This approach—taken by both Sol LeWitt and Sigurd Lewerentz—of defining a rule and then following it regardless of its consequences really strikes me. In my opinion it implies a design strategy very close to Karl Popper's concept of falsifiability: in order to verify your proposition you need to stress it to its limits.

> In your USM masterclass, you looked at modular forms of organic growth and used a tree-like structure as a model for your architectural constructions. What made you interested in this approach?

LB   At a certain point we realized that we could use nature as a metaphor. So we started to observe nature and the way plants grow, identifying the relationship between the different parts of a tree on a very small scale but also within the wider landscape. We thought this could be an interesting way of investigating modularity, allowing us to consider the issue from a very broad perspective.

> Do we find modularity in the branches of a tree because it is actually there, or do you think it's because we already have modularity in mind and are looking in a certain way?

LB   If we consider the question almost philosophically, trees are modular but also unconscious. For a tree, modularity is not even an issue. Vegetation develops out of necessity, as a reaction to its surrounding environment, and perhaps for reasons that are still unknown to us. So we perceive modularity in trees and vegetation because we are looking for it. I guess it's a bit like watching clouds and seeing figures in them. It's the psychological process of seeing something vague and yet perceiving something significant.

1   Sol LeWitt, 'Sentences on Conceptual Art', *Art Language*, i/I (1969).

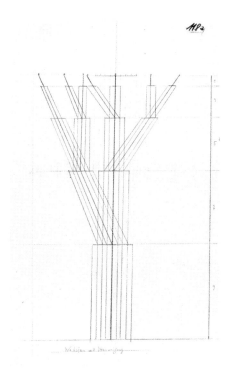

Paul Klee, 'Bildnerische Gestaltungslehre II.
19 Progressionen', 1923–31

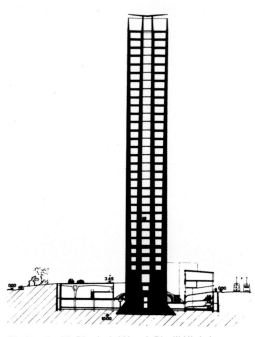

Gio Ponti with Pier Luigi Nervi, Pirelli Highrise,
drawing, 1958

Presentation by Lorenzo Bini's masterclass
at the Domaine de Boisbuchet, France, 2014

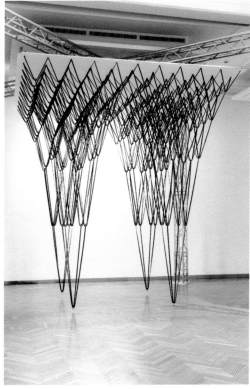

Lorenzo Bini's masterclass, 'TreeD',
exhibition view in Milan, 2015

'rethink the modular', exhibition view in Milan, 2015

Your starting point for this masterclass was to investigate patterns that could be read in nature. With that in mind, do you consider your understanding of modularity as a counterpoint to an architecture influenced by organic formal principles?

LB   When we use the expression 'organic formal principles' to describe certain buildings—or the body of work produced by certain architects—the adjective 'formal' is much more relevant for me than 'organic'. The word 'organic' indicates an attempt to give dignity to a 'formal' approach, which is generally considered unbecoming. I have the feeling that both expressions belong to architectural criticism rather than architectural practice. Another word with negative connotations I used to employ very often in architectural discussions is 'arbitrary'. Nevertheless, I've recently understood that even arbitrary acts, gestures or forms can become good architecture— as long as designers develop them logically.

In what ways do you think your observations on the modular character of nature could influence your architectural practice? Might they affect the way you think of the structures themselves? Are you trying to define a new functionalism?

LB   No, absolutely not! When we were asked to 'rethink the modular' for the masterclass, looking at nature seemed a very logical step, and that's about it. My architectural practice is completely missing any kind of programmatic element. There are different reasons for this, but more and more I think that, if I had that ambition, my profession would become boring. There are things I learned, things I know, things I trust, things I like and things I am curious about … But I struggle to forget them all the time and to discover new things in every project. I would be extremely happy if the attitude of the Spanish writer Javier Marías could be transferred into architectural practice. In an interview for the *Paris Review* he said: 'I work without a map. I work only with a compass, which means that I know more or less where I am going. It's not that I just wander nonsensically in a totally whimsical way. I probably find the same river and the same desert and the same cliffs and the same precipice that the other writers find, but I find them

unexpectedly. I like not to know everything.'[2]
That's a risky attitude even for writers—and
architects are required to plan and control
everything. Then again, is 'wandering with a
compass' already a programmatic statement?

II It's striking that your work seems to reflect the
discussion you've led from the very beginning of
your masterclass, about opposing standardization
and uniformity, and the flexibility of a modular
system. It reminds me of the discussion between
Le Corbusier and Walter Gropius, who used a very
beautiful term: 'organic modularity'. Looking around
the exhibition here in Milan, you see all these updates
on the notion of modularity, and how important
the role of nature is to many works. It's a system, but
it's a natural system.

LB There is so much you can learn from nature.
That's why we observed trees with this specific
theme in mind. You might say that there is a kind of
opposition between standardization and nature but,
when we were asked to rethink modularity, we pretty
soon realized that modularity is not just about the
repetition of standardizing elements, especially when
applied to architecture. We understood modularity
as something that has a lot to do with proportion
and scale. When you talk about modularity,
you immediately invoke the relationship between
different elements and different scales, as well
as the relationship between human proportions and
the scale of buildings. The lesson you can learn
from trees is that they also have similar proportional
relationships between their different parts. In this
respect the greatest achievement of our research is the
notion that trees are modular, because there is always
a geometrical, dimensional or structural relationship
between one branch and another, or between one
part of the tree and another. And the amazing thing
is that's completely unconscious: they just develop
that way.

2    *Paris Review*, no. 179 (Winter 2006),
     http://www.theparisreview.org/inter-
     views/5680/the-art-of-fiction- no-190-
     javier-marias [last accessed 13 May 2015].

Lorenzo Bini, one of the tutors of seven USM
masterclasses, was interviewed during the 'rethink
the modular' workshop at the Domaine de Boisbuchet,
France, 2014 (I), and on the occasion of the 'rethink
the modular' exhibition in Milan, 2015 (II).

# A Retrospective of USM Haller

The following pages present a selection of historical photographs that reflect USM's corporate communications over the course of five decades. The company began by specializing in window-fitting. After World War II it focused on industrial building systems, constructing its own factory from 1961 to 1964. The registration of the USM ball joint in 1965 opened new perspectives: USM Modular Furniture Haller was born, allowing for creative office planning from the late 1960s. Since the 1990s USM Haller has also made its mark in the residential sector.

# 1980s

9

9 USM Haller, customized
  private bank interior,
  Nuremberg, 1986
10 USM Haller, customized
  bank interior, 1985
11 USM Haller, open-plan
  architects' office, US, 1982

10

11

# 1990s

12  USM Haller / USM Kitos,
    meeting area, 1996
13  USM Haller, bar storage, 1990s
14  USM Haller, office with
    welcome desk, 1993

12

13

14

# 1960s

1

2

1 USM production facilities,
 Münsingen, Switzerland, 1963
2 USM Haller ball joint, 1965
3 USM Headquarters, office
 building, Münsingen,
 Switzerland, 1960s
4 USM production facilities,
 Münsingen, Switzerland,
 *c.* 1967

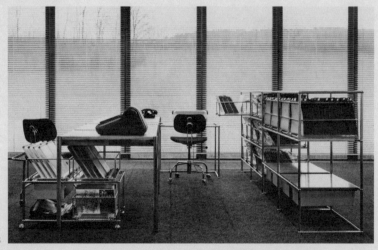

3

4

# 1970s

5

6

8

7

5   USM Haller, file storage, 1970
     product catalogue
6   USM Haller, 'Teamland',
     open-plan office concept,
     Zurich, 1973
7   USM Headquarters,
     Münsingen, Switzerland,
     1969
8   USM Haller, welcome desk,
     1976

# 2000s

15

16

15   USM Haller, pharmaceutical
     storage, Biel, Switzerland,
     2008
16   USM Haller, media unit,
     New York, 2007
17   USM Haller, open-plan
     office, Cologne, 2001

17

# 2010s

18

19

18　USM Haller, bedside table, 2010
19　USM Haller, bookshelves, 2010
20　USM Haller, project50 advertising campaign, 2015

20

# Contributors' Biographies

DIMITRI BÄHLER studied product design at the École Cantonale d'Art de Lausanne (ECAL) with an exchange at the Design Academy in Eindhoven. Based in Biel/Bienne in Switzerland, he works for galleries such as NOV in Geneva and Kissthedesign in Lausanne, as well as for international companies such as HAY and Moustache. In 2013 his work *Patterns & Colors* was selected as part of the *Design Parade 8* exhibition at the Villa Noailles in Hyères, France, and was nominated for the Swiss Design Award in 2014.

LORENZO BINI was educated at the Politecnico di Milano and at the Statens Håndverks- og Kunstindustriskole in Oslo. Between 2000 and 2003 he worked as a senior architect for West8 Urban Design & Landscape Architecture in the Netherlands. In 2003 he co-founded and directed studiometrico in Milan, working there until 2011, after which he started a new practice called Binocle. Lorenzo Bini has taught at the Politecnico di Milano for the past ten years and was visiting professor at the Design Academy of Eindhoven. He was awarded first prize in the ArchDaily Building of the Year competition in 2009 for studiometrico's project 'bastard store' in the Interiors category. His work has appeared in *Total Office Design* (2011), *Out of the Box!* (2011) and *Re-use Architecture* (2011), among other publications.

BLESS is a fashion and design studio created in 1997 by Ines Kaag, based in Berlin, and Desiree Heiss, living in Paris. The two designers avoid any calibrated definition of fashion. Their product collections have been presented in various exhibition contexts around the world, including the 2nd Istanbul

Design Biennial (2014), the MAK Fashion Lab #1 (2013) and the Tel Aviv Museum of Art (2012). Their work was also honoured with the Ars Viva Art and Design Award, Germany (2001), the Andam Award, France (1999 and 2004) and the Outstanding Artist Award, Austria (2014). Since 2006 they have taught product design at the HfG Karlsruhe, Germany.

DR THOMAS DIENES is Head of Group Product Development at USM U. Schärer Söhne AG in Münsingen, Switzerland. He graduated in architecture at the University of Karlsruhe under Fritz Haller, and was awarded a PhD at the Vienna University of Technology. He worked as the chair of constructional engineering and conception at the University of Karlsruhe, was a business partner at Dienes and Leichtle, and was head of the Fraunhofer Office Innovation Center in Stuttgart. He has worked at USM Switzerland since 2010.

GO HASEGAWA was born in 1977 in Saitama, Japan. He studied under Yoshiharu Tsukamoto at the Tokyo Institute of Technology and worked for Taira Nishizawa architects before establishing his own practice, Go Hasegawa & Associates, in 2005. His first monograph, *Go Hasegawa Works*, was published in 2012. He was awarded the Kajima Prize in 2005 for 'Pilotis in the Forest', and the AR Design Vanguard Prize in 2014. He has taught at the Tokyo Institute of Technology since 2009 and the Accademia di Architettura, Mendrisio, since 2012.

REM KOOLHAAS is a Dutch architect, architectural theorist and urbanist, and is Professor of the Practice of Architecture and Urban Design at the Graduate School of Design, Harvard University. He studied at the Netherlands Film and Television Academy in Amsterdam, the Architectural Association School of Architecture, London, and Cornell University, Ithaca, New York. He is the founding partner of the Office for Metropolitan Architecture (OMA) and its research-oriented counterpart AMO, both in Rotterdam. In 2005 he co-founded *Volume Magazine* together with Mark Wigley and Ole Bouman. As an author, Koolhaas has published *Delirious New York* (1978), *S, M, L, XL* (1995) and *Project Japan: Metabolism Talks* (2011), among other titles. In 2000 Koolhaas was awarded the Pritzker Prize, and in 2014 he curated the 14th Venice Architecture Biennale.

THOMAS LOMMÉE studied at the Design Academy in Eindhoven, ENSCI Les Ateliers in Paris and the Institute without Boundaries in Toronto. He then went on to establish Intrastructures in 2007: a pragmatic, utopian design studio that emphasizes the physical, digital and social contexts of product design. He is initiator of the OpenStructures project, which has been shown at the Z33 House for Contemporary Art, Hasselt, Belgium, and elsewhere. In addition to his activities as a designer and design researcher, Lommée has taught at the Design Academy Eindhoven and is the co-founder of the ENSCImatique project at ENSCI Les Ateliers in Paris. He lives and works in Brussels.

WOLF MANGELSDORF graduated from Karlsruhe University with a degree in architecture and civil engineering, having studied under Fritz Haller. He joined BuroHappold in 2002 and has since been made a partner. He heads up the London structural engineering team. Mangelsdorf has worked with world-renowned architects on iconic structures in the United Kingdom and elsewhere. Since 2000 he has taught at the Architectural Association in London and has been a guest lecturer and tutor at a number of universities around the world.

JÜRGEN MAYER H. is the founder of J. Mayer H. Architects. He studied at Stuttgart University, the Cooper Union, New York, and Princeton University. His work has been published and exhibited worldwide and is held in numerous private and public collections, including the Museum of Modern Art, New York, and the San Francisco Museum of Art. His national and international awards include a special mention for the Mies van der Rohe Award in 2003, the Holcim Bronze Award in 2005 and the Audi Urban Future Award in 2010. Jürgen Mayer H. has taught at Princeton University, Harvard University and the Architectural Association in London, among other institutions.

BURKHARD MELTZER worked in the curatorial team of the Neue Kunst Halle St. Gallen from 2003 to 2007, as a curatorial assistant until 2006, and as a curator and director until 2007. He has been a lecturer and researcher at the Zurich University of the Arts (ZHdK) since 2006. He has also worked as a freelance curator and has written for publications such as *Kunstbulletin*, *Frieze* magazine and *Spike*. In addition Meltzer has co-edited books and magazines including *It's Not a Garden Table: Art and Design in the Expanded Field* (2011) and *Design Exhibited* (2013).

DR ALVA NOË received his PhD from Harvard in 1995 and is Professor of Philosophy at the University of California, Berkeley, where he is also a member of the Institute for Cognitive and Brain Sciences and the Center for New Media. He was previously Distinguished Professor of Philosophy at the Graduate Center of the City University of New York, and has been philosopher-in-residence with the Forsythe Company, a dance group based in Frankfurt. He is the author of *Action in Perception* (2004), *Out of Our Heads* (2009) and *Varieties of Presence* (2012). He received a Guggenheim Fellowship in 2012 and is a former fellow of the Institute for Advanced Study, Berlin.

HANS ULRICH OBRIST is co-director of the Serpentine Galleries, London. Prior to this, he was curator of the Musée d'Art Moderne, Paris. He has curated the *Kitchen Show* at his St. Gallen apartment (1991), Manifesta I (1995), the 50th Venice Biennale (2003) and the Lyon Biennal (2007), among other exhibitions. He co-curates the Serpentine Gallery Pavilions, a series of temporary structures at the Serpentine Gallery, and the Marathon series of events. He has given lectures at both academic and art institutions around the world, including the European Graduate School in Switzerland, the Institute of Historical Research at the University of London, and the Architectural Association School of Architecture, also in London.

TIDO VON OPPELN works as an author and curator in Zurich. Since 2005 he has been involved in several exhibitions on design, art and architecture at the Werkbundarchiv – Museum der Dinge, Berlin, the Vitra Design Museum in

Weil am Rhein, the Marta Herford Modern Art Museum and the MuseumsQuartier in Vienna. He writes for various design magazines, including the Belgian art, architecture and design magazine *DAMN*. Since 2009 he has lectured on design theory and history at Lucerne University of Applied Sciences and Arts (HSLU) and at Zurich University of the Arts (ZHdK). In addition von Oppeln collaborates with Burkhard Meltzer on joint research and exhibition projects, as well as publications including *It's Not a Garden Table: Art and Design in the Expanded Field* (2011) and *Design Exhibited* (2013).

NATHALIE DU PASQUIER is a French-born artist and designer. She was a founding member of the influential and decade-defining Memphis Group along with Ettore Sottsass and others, creating patterns for textiles and furniture. Despite her design success, in 1987 she shifted her focus to her fine art practice and painting in particular. She has exhibited in numerous group and solo shows in galleries and museums throughout Europe, China and the United States.

RICK POYNOR is an author who specializes in design, graphic design and visual culture. He has co-founded several specialist magazines such as *Eye* and the online journal *design-observer*. Poynor also works as a visiting Professor of Art and Design Criticism at the Royal College of Art, London. His publications include *Design without Boundaries* (1998), *No More Rules: Graphic Design and Postmodernism* (2003) and *Multiple Signatures* (2013).

DR CATHARINE ROSSI is Senior Lecturer in Design History at Kingston University, London, where her areas

of research include post-war Italian design, contemporary design and craft, and ethically engaged approaches to design, both past and present. In 2014 Rossi was invited to curate *Space Electronic: Then and Now* at the 2014 Venice Architecture Biennale. She co-edited *The Italian Avant-Garde: 1968–1976* (2013) with Alex Coles, and in 2015 she published *Crafting Design in Italy*. Rossi has contributed to various magazines including *Crafts*, *Disegno* and *Domus*. She was a nominator for the 2014 and 2015 Design of the Year awards for the Design Museum, London.

DR ANTONIO SCARPONI is an Italian architect and designer who studied architecture at Cooper Union, New York, and IUAV University in Venice, which awarded him a PhD in urban design. He conceives small-scale strategic interventions that he defines as 'conceptual devices' – which is also the name of his practice. Believing that food plays a central role in resilient contemporary urban developments, he has designed several urban agricultural projects, conceived as a way to 'grow the city'. In 2013 he published an instruction manual for a piece of furniture that does not exist: called ELIOOO, it is a hydroponic system to grow food at home using IKEA parts. In 2008 Antonio Scarponi was awarded the Curry Stone Design Prize.

JERSZY SEYMOUR was born in Berlin and grew up in London, where he graduated in engineering design from South Bank Polytechnic in 1989, and in industrial design from the Royal College of Art in 1994. His work has been shown at the Vitra Design Museum (*Living Systems*, 2007) and the MAK in Vienna (*The First Supper*,

2008). In 2000 he was presented with the Dedalus Award for European Design, and he received the Taro Okamoto Memorial Award for Contemporary Art in 2003. In 2011 Seymour initiated and assumed direction of the programme known as the Dirty Art Department, the new Applied Art and Design Master's course at the Sandberg Institute of the Rietveld Academy, Amsterdam. His first solo exhibition, *The Universe Wants To Play*, opened at the Galerie Crone, Berlin, in 2013.

DR MARTINO STIERLI is the Philip Johnson Chief Curator of Architecture and Design at the Museum of Modern Art, New York. He is also Swiss National Science Foundation Professor at the Institute of Art History at the University of Zurich. Stierli is the author of *Las Vegas in the Rearview Mirror: The City in Theory, Photography, and Film* (2013) and co-curator of the international travelling exhibition *Las Vegas Studio*. His research focuses on architecture and media, urban images, the representation of space and the genealogy of postmodernism.

JOHN THACKARA is a writer, philosopher and event producer who, over the last three decades, has travelled the world looking for examples of what a sustainable future could be like. He writes about these stories at his blog Doorsofperception.com. He has published several books, including *Design After Modernism: Beyond the Object (1988)*, *In the Bubble: Designing in a Complex World* (2006) and *How to Thrive in the Next Economy* (2015). Thackara teaches at the Royal College of Art, London, and at Mushashino Art University in Tokyo, and is a visiting professor at the School of Visual Arts in New York. He is also a member of the Design Commission of the UK Parliament.

DR GEORG VRACHLIOTIS is Professor for Theory of Architecture at the Karlsruhe Institute of Technology (KIT), and previously lectured and conducted research at the Institute for History and Theory of Architecture and the Institute of Technology in Architecture at ETH Zurich. He co-edited *Structuralism Reloaded: Rule-Based Design in Architecture and Urbanism* (2011) and several publications in the Kontext Architektur series (2008–10). Since 2014 he has been head of the Archive for Architecture and Engineering in Southwest Germany (SAAI).

ALLAN WEXLER has worked in the fields of architecture, design and fine art for over forty-five years. He teaches at the School of Constructed Environments at Parsons The New School for Design, New York. Wexler's works explore human activity and the built environment. They have been shown in various museums, including the San Francisco Museum of Modern Art, the Contemporary Art Center in Cincinnati and the Forum for Contemporary Art in St. Louis. His work *Crate House* (1990) is part of the permanent collection of the Osthaus Museum in Hagen, Germany. Wexler is represented by the Ronald Feldman Gallery in New York.

## PHOTOGRAPHIC CREDITS

All works of art and documentary photographs are reproduced by kind permission of the owners. As far as possible, the editors have contacted the copyright owners of the images used in this publication. In cases where this has not been possible we apologize and request the copyright owners to contact the editor or the publisher. Specific acknowledgments are as follows:

p. 4: ↖ Fritz Haller, 'Properties of Particular Points of Regular Geometric Systems', 1967–68, ©gta Archives/ETH Zurich (Holding Fritz Haller); → Frei Otto/Larry Medlin, Model for a convertible roof, German Pavilion, Montreal, 1964, ©saai, Südwestdeutsches Archiv für Architektur und Ingenieurbau, Karlsruhe Institut für Technologie, Werkarchiv Frei Otto, Photo: saai, Martin Kunz ↙ Jerszy Seymour, 'Workshop Chair', 2009, ©Jerszy Seymour Archive
p. 5 ↗ Bless masterclass, 'Exoteric Souvenirs', 2014–15, Photo: Anne Morgenstern ↙ Go Hasegawa masterclass, 'Hole', 2014, Photo: Anne Morgenstern

p. 11: ©gta Archives/ETH Zurich (Holding Fritz Haller)
p. 12: ©2015, ProLitteris, Zurich, courtesy FRAC Centre, Orléans
p. 15: ↑©USM U. Schärer Söhne AG, Photo: Rolf Frei; ←©Nathalie du Pasquier, ©Victoria and Albert Museum, London

pp. 17–22
1: ©2015, ProLitteris, Zurich
2: ©saai, Südwestdeutsches Archiv für Architektur und Ingenieurbau, Karlsruher Institut für Technologie, Werkarchiv Frei Otto, Photo: saai, Martin Kunz
3: ©gta Archives/ETH Zurich (Holding Fritz Haller)
4: ©gta Archives/ETH Zurich (Holding Fritz Haller), Photo: Therese Beyeler
5: ©Allan Wexler
6: ©BuroHappold Engineering
7: Photo: Celia Torvisco, Alexandre d'Orsetti
8: Provided courtesy of Safdie Architects, Photo: Jerry Spearman
9: ©gta Archives/ETH Zurich (Holding Fritz Haller)
10: ©Jerszy Seymour Archive
11: ©Nathalie du Pasquier

pp. 24–25: Mass Studies, 'Seoul Commune 2026', 2005, courtesy of Mass Studies

pp. 33–35: Thomas Lommée with Jo Van Bostraeten & Andrea De Chirico, OpenStructures (OS) 'CargoBike 2.0', 2013; Thomas Lommée at the USM masterclass workshop, 2014, Photos: Anne Morgenstern
p. 36: Photos: Celia Torvisco, Alexandre d'Orsetti
pp. 37–38: Photos: Anne Morgenstern
p. 40: ↖↗←↙ Lukas Wegwerth for OpenStructures (OS), Photo: Catherine Lommée; → Kirstie Van Noort for OpenStructures (OS), Photo: Catherine Lommée; ↘ Fabio Lorefice for OpenStructures (OS), Photo: Catherine Lommée
p. 41: ↖ Fabio Lorefice for OpenStructures (OS), Photo: Catherine Lommée; ↗←→ Lukas Wegwerth for OpenStructures (OS), Photo: Catherine Lommée; ↙ Marianne Cardon for OpenStructures (OS), Photo: Catherine Lommée; ↘ Dries Verbruggen for OpenStructures (OS), Photo: Catherine Lommée

pp. 44–45: Jerszy Seymour, 'Coalition of Amateurs', Mudam Luxembourg, 2009, ©Jerszy Seymour Archive
p. 49: ©Nathalie du Pasquier with Ajumi Han for Bodum®, Photo: Anne Morgenstern
pp. 50–51: ©Nathalie du Pasquier, Photo: Delfino Sisto Legnani
p. 53: ↑Photo: Monica Tarocco; ↓Produced by daskonzept, Photo: Antonio Scarponi
pp. 54–55: ©Jerszy Seymour Archive

pp. 58–59: Dave Hakkens, Phonebloks modular components, 2013, ©Phonebloks
p. 61: ©Phonebloks
pp. 62–67: Photos: Anne Morgenstern
p. 69: ©Alex Goad

p. 71: Wolf Mangelsdorf at the USM masterclass workshop, 2014; Wolf Mangelsdorf masterclass, working model, 2014, Photos: Anne Morgenstern
p. 74: Provided courtesy of Safdie Architects, Photo: Jerry Spearman
p. 75: Provided courtesy of Safdie Architects, Photo: Timothy Hursley
p. 77: ↑©saai, Südwestdeutsches Archiv für Architektur und Ingenieurbau, Karlsruher Institut für Technologie, Werkarchiv Günter Behnisch and Partner, Photo: Christian Kandzia; ↓©BuroHappold Engineering, Photo: Mandy Reynolds
p. 78: ↓©Bundesarchiv, Germany, Bild 183–E0607–0005–002, Photo: Helmut Schaar

pp. 86–87: Fritz Haller, System control for study, Integral Urban, a Global Model, 1975, ©gta Archives/ETH Zurich (Holding Fritz Haller)
pp. 90–91: ©gta Archives/ETH Zurich (Holding Fritz Haller), Photos: Christian Moser
pp. 92–95: ©gta Archives/ETH Zurich (Holding Fritz Haller)
p. 96: Arata Isozaki & Associates
p. 97: ↑©Courtesy FRAC Centre, Orléans, Photo: Philippe Magnon; ↓©gta Archives/ETH Zurich (Holding Fritz Haller)
p. 98: ©Yona Friedman
p. 100: ©gta Archives/ETH Zurich (Holding Fritz Haller)
p. 101: ↑©2015 The Museum of Modern Art, New York/Scala, Florence; ↓©USM U. Schärer Söhne AG
p. 103: ©J. Mayer H. Architects

pp. 105–07: Allan Wexler at the USM masterclass workshop, 2014; Allan Wexler masterclass, presentation at the Domaine de Boisbuchet, France, 2014, Photos: Anne Morgenstern
p. 108: ©Allan Wexler
pp. 110–13: ©Allan Wexler
p. 115: Photo: Anne Morgenstern
pp. 116–17: ©Allan Wexler

pp. 119–24
1: ©Superstudio, Photo: Cristiano Toraldo di Francia
2: Photo: Anne Morgenstern
3: ©USM U. Schärer Söhne AG
4: ©USM U. Schärer Söhne AG, Photo: Rolf Frei
5: ©Matteo Thun, Photo: Anne Morgenstern
6: ©Cini Boeri Architetti Archive, Photo: Masera
7: Courtesy Gae Aulenti Studio
8: ©Gio Ponti Archives, Salvatore Licitra
9: ©USM U. Schärer Söhne AG, Photo: Daniel Sutter
10: ©J. Mayer H. Architects
11: ©USM U. Schärer Söhne AG
12: Photo: Anne Morgenstern

pp. 126–27: ©Superstudio, 'Misura furniture', 1969, Photo: Cristiano Toraldo di Francia
p. 131: ©Superstudio
p. 132: ©Superstudio, Photos: Cristiano Toraldo di Francia
p. 135: ©Superstudio
pp. 136–37: ©Archizoom Associati/Archivio Andrea Branzi, courtesy FRAC Centre, Orléans, Photo: Philippe Magnon
p. 141: ↑©Courtesy of Gae Aulenti Studio; ↓©Superstudio, Photo: Cristiano Toraldo di Francia
pp. 142–43: ©Courtesy of Gae

Aulenti Studio, Photo: Valerio Castelli
p. 146: ↑ Ignazia Favata / Studio Joe Colombo, Photo: Valerio Castelli; ↓ Cini Boeri Architetti Archive, Photo: Masera
p. 147: © 2015, ProLitteris, Zurich
p. 149: © Superstudio
p. 150: Photos: Courtesy of Richard Sapper
p. 151: ↑ © Superstudio, Photo: Cristiano Toraldo di Francia; ↓ © Superstudio

p. 155: Bless masterclass at work, Domaine de Boisbuchet, France, 2014; Bless masterclass, presentation at the Domaine de Boisbuchet, France, 2014, Photos: Anne Morgenstern
p. 157: ← © Bless, Photo: Tim Schroeder; → © Bless
pp. 160–65: Photos: Anne Morgenstern

pp. 168–69: USM Modular Furniture Haller, advertising photograph, 1976, © USM U. Schärer Söhne AG, Photo: Rolf Frei, Concept: Roberto Medici
p. 172: USM U. Schärer Söhne AG
p. 174: ↑ © Rüegg-Naegeli AG, Zurich; ↓ © USM U. Schärer Söhne AG
pp. 176–81: © USM U. Schärer Söhne AG, Photos: Rolf Frei
pp. 182–83: © Jaime Ardiles-Arce
p. 185: © USM U. Schärer Söhne AG
p. 187: © USM U. Schärer Söhne AG, ↑ Photo: Axel Bleyer; ↓ Photo: Bruno Augsburger

pp. 188–89: Seoul Skyline, 2015, Photo: Adam Dean
p. 192: © Office for Metropolitan Architecture (OMA), Photo: Iwan Baan
pp. 194–97: © Office for Metropolitan Architecture (OMA)
p. 199: ↑ © Office for Metropolitan Architecture (OMA), Photo: Philippe Ruault; ↓ © Cedric Price Fonds, Collection Centre Canadien d'Architecture/Canadian Centre for Architecture, Montreal
p. 200–01: © Office for Metropolitan Architecture (OMA), Photo: Philippe Ruault
p. 203: © Courtesy Ed van der Elsken, Nederlands Fotomuseum, Annet Gelink Gallery
p. 206: Deutsches Architekturmuseum, Frankfurt a. M.

p. 209: Go Hasegawa at the USM masterclass workshop, 2014; Go Hasegawa masterclass, 'Hole', 2014, Photos: Anne Morgenstern
p. 210: © Go Hasegawa & Associates, Photo: Iwan Baan
p. 211: Photo: Anne Morgenstern

p. 212: © Go Hasegawa & Associates
p. 213: © Go Hasegawa & Associates, Photo: Takumi Ota
p. 214: © Go Hasegawa & Associates
p. 217: Photos: Anne Morgenstern

pp. 220–21: Go Hasegawa masterclass, presentation at the Domaine de Boisbuchet, France, 2014, Photo: Anne Morgenstern

p. 237: Dimitri Bähler at the USM masterclass workshop, 2014; Dimitri Bähler masterclass, working model, 2014, Photos: Anne Morgenstern
p. 239–41: Photos: Anne Morgenstern
p. 243: ↑ © Dimitri Bähler; ↓ © Courtesy Dimitri Bähler, EKWC
pp. 244–49: Photos: Anne Morgenstern

pp. 250–51: © J. Mayer H. Architects, anti-governement demonstration under the Metropol Parasol, Seville, 2011, © J. Mayer H. Architects, Photo: Fernando Alda
p. 254–55: © J. Mayer H. Architects, Photos: Fernando Alda;
p. 258: © USM U. Schärer Söhne AG, Photo: Björn Ewers, Studio314, Berlin
pp. 260–61: © Elemental
p. 262: ↑ © Elemental, Photo: Tadeuz Jalocha; ↓ © Elemental, Photo: Cristobal Palma / Estudio Palma;
p. 263: © Elemental, Photo: Cristobal Palma / Estudio Palma
p. 265: © J. Mayer H. Architects, Photo: Ludger Paffrath for Euroboden
p. 266: ↖ ↗ © Kisho Kurokawa architect & associates; ↓ © Kisho Kurokawa architect & associates, Photo: Tomio Ohashi
p. 267: © Kisho Kurokawa architect & associates

p. 271: Lorenzo Bini at the Domaine de Boisbuchet, France, 2014, Photo: Anne Morgenstern; Bruno Munari, Drawing from Disegnare un Albero, 1978, © Bruno Munari. All rights reserved to Maurizio Corraini srl. Mantova
p. 273: © Lorenzo Bini, Photo: Francesca Pozzi; p. 275: © Lorenzo Bini, Photos: Giovanna Silva
p. 276: ↑ © 2015, ProLitteris, Zurich; ↓ © Sigurd Lewerentz, Photo: Anders Clausson, 2015
p. 277: © 2015, ProLitteris, Zurich, The Noguchi Museum, New York;
p. 279: ↖ Coloured pencil and pencil on paper (verso), 33 × 21 cm, Zentrum Paul Klee, Bern, Archives, inv. no. BG II.19/89; ↗ © Gio Ponti Archives – Salvatore Licitra;
↙ ↘ Photos: Anne Morgenstern
pp. 280–81: Anne Morgenstern

pp. 285–90
1: © gta Archives / ETH Zurich (Holding Fritz Haller)
2: © USM U. Schärer Söhne AG
3: © gta Archives / ETH Zurich (Holding Fritz Haller), Photo: Alfred Hablützel
4: © gta Archives / ETH Zurich (Holding Fritz Haller), Photo: Christian Moser
5: © USM U. Schärer Söhne AG
6: © Rüegg-Naegeli AG, Zurich
7–10: © USM U. Schärer Söhne AG
11: © Jaime Ardiles-Arce
12–16: © USM U. Schärer Söhne AG, Photo: Bruno Augsburger
17: © USM U. Schärer Söhne AG, Photo: Daniel Sutter
18: © USM U. Schärer Söhne AG, Photo: Miloby Ideasystem
19: © USM U. Schärer Söhne AG, Photo: Daniel Sutter
20: © USM U. Schärer Söhne AG, Photo: Lukas Wassmann

Cover
From left to right:
1: © 2015, ProLitteris, Zurich
2: Photo: Martin Adam/Berlin
3: © Atelier Frei Otto+Partner, Deutsches Architekturmuseum, Frankfurt am Main
4: Courtesy of Gae Aulenti Studio, Photo: Valerio Castelli
5: Courtesy Nathalie du Pasquier, © Bodum Design Group
6: Photo: Anne Morgenstern
7: © USM U. Schärer Söhne AG, Photo: Rolf Frei
8: © gta Archives / ETH Zurich (Holding Fritz Haller)

PUBLICATION

This publication was initiated by USM as part of the 'rethink the modular' cultural initiative on the occasion of the 50th anniversary of USM Modular Furniture Haller.

## USM

To find out more, please visit **www.usm.com**.

Editors on behalf of USM:
Burkhard Meltzer, Tido von Oppeln

Editorial coordination, text and picture editing:
Giulia Stoll

Interviewers for 'rethink the modular':
Rick Poynor, Max Borka, Tido von Oppeln, Burkhard Meltzer, Giulia Stoll, Anna Kaminsky

Translation from German:
Brian Currid

Special thanks to:
Rick Poynor, Max Borka, Catharine Rossi, Christian Müller and Kurt Breiter (2bm architekten, Solothurn), Filine Wagner (gta Archives / ETH Zurich), Georg Vrachliotis, Therese Beyeler, Roberto Medici, Urs Stampfli

USM MASTERCLASSES

Workshop at the Domaine de Boisbuchet, France, 14–21 September 2014

Workshop coordination:
Giulia Stoll

Tutors and participants:
Dimitri Bähler (ECAL / Ecole cantonale d'art de Lausanne) Sylvain Aebischer, Joelle Aeschlimann, Manuel Amaral Netto, Marie Douel, Valentine Dubois, Sarha Duquesne, Christophe Guberan, Linn Kandel, Yann Mathys, Mathieu Rivier, Pauline Saglio

Lorenzo Bini (Politecnico di Milano) Alice Colombo, Maria Elena Garzoni, Elisa Mansutti, Ludovica Niero, Anna Pierotello, Eugenio Pizzo

Bless (Hochschule für Gestaltung, Karlsruhe)
Christina Becker, Denis Bulut, Lisa Ertel, Pia Mareike Matthes, Marlene Oeken, Sonja Rogova, Philipp Scholz, Martha Schwindling

Go Hasegawa
(Tokyo Institute of Technology) Shun Hayasaka, Shunpei Ichikawa, Sho Kurokawa, Yuto Makishima, Tomoya Nishimura, Yuki Nobukawa, Saori Toyoshima

Thomas Lommée
(ENSCI les Ateliers, Paris)
Maud Bausier, Florian Bédé, Sylvain Chassériaux, Céline Coq, Antoine Giret, Maxime Loiseau, Fanny Muller, Alexandre d'Orsetti, Fanny Serouart, Celia Torvisco

Wolf Mangelsdorf
(Architectural Association School of Architecture, London)
Zeynep Aksoz, Joe Allberry, Amritha Krishnan, Lucas Mory, Nikul Vadgama, Daniel Zaldivar

Allan Wexler
(Parsons The New School for Design, New York City)
Zachary Barr, Benjamin Billick, Kelsey Coyle, Elmar Fujita, Miriam Josi, Michael David Lee, Molly Page, Stella Lee Prowse

Observer:
Rick Poynor

EXHIBITION

'rethink the modular', exhibition at the Salone dei Tessuti, Milan, 14–19 April 2015

Curators:
(USM masterclasses and exhibition) Burkhard Meltzer, Tido von Oppeln

Exhibition coordination:
Christoph Blaas

Exhibition design:
Annika von Oppeln

Graphic design:
Atlas Studio

USM masterclasses led by:
Dimitri Bähler
Lorenzo Bini
Bless
Go Hasegawa
Thomas Lommée
Wolf Mangelsdorf
Allan Wexler

Works by:
Volker Albus
Archigram
Yona Friedman
Fritz Haller
Trix & Robert Haussmann
Hans Hollein
Nathalie du Pasquier
Ettore Sottsass
Superstudio
Matteo Thun

Lenders:
Archive Hans Hollein, Vienna
ETH Library, Zurich
Fredi Fischli, Zurich
gta Archives / ETH Zurich
(Holding Fritz Haller)
MAXXI Museo nazionale delle Arti del XXI secolo, Rome

The editors of this book would like to thank Alexander Schärer (CEO/ Owner) and Stéphanie Borge (Group Marketing Director) who have supported the 'rethink the modular' initiative from the very first day. The overall anniversary campaign, 'project50', was conceived by Lukas Frei (Creative Director) and Michèle Gutmann (Project Lead) of Scholz and Friends, Switzerland.

Excerpt from "Wide Minds" from *Out of Our Heads: Why You Are Not Your Brain, and Other Lessons from the Biology of Consciousness* by Alva Noë. Copyright © 2009 by Alva Noë. Reprinted by permission of Hill and Wang, an imprint of Farrar, Straus and Giroux, LLC.

Excerpt from "Dynamic Labyrinth (Seoul)" from *Rem Koolhaas and Hans Ulrich Obrist: The Conversation Series.* Copyright © 2006 Rem Koolhaas, Hans Ulrich Obrist and Verlag der Buchhandlung Walther König. Reprinted by permission of Verlag der Buchhandlung Walther König.

First published in the United Kingdom in 2016 by Thames & Hudson Ltd, 181A High Holborn London WC1V 7QX

*Rethinking the Modular* © 2016 USM U. Schärer Söhne AG

Designed by Atlas Studio

All Rights Reserved. No part of this publication may be reproduced or transmitted in any form or by any means, electronic or mechanical, including photocopy, recording or any other information storage and retrieval system, without prior permission in writing from the publisher.

British Library Cataloguing-in-Publication Data
A catalogue record for this book is available from the British Library

ISBN 978-0-500-29235-8

Printed and bound in China by C & C Offset Printing Co. Ltd

To find out about all our publications, please visit **www.thamesandhudson.com.** There you can subscribe to our e-newsletter, browse or download our current catalogue, and buy any titles that are in print.